Performing
WOODEN
TOYS

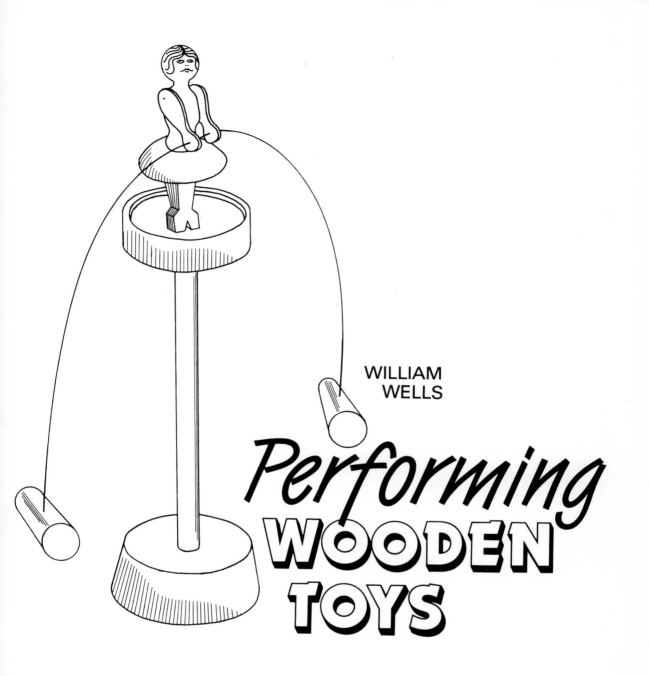

WILLIAM
WELLS

Performing
WOODEN
TOYS

B. T. BATSFORD LTD · LONDON

Acknowledgment

Grateful thanks to my wife, Jenny, for her patience and help with the typing, and to John Lundy for his invaluable help with the illustrations.

ISBN 0 7134 4721 4

Typeset by Chelmsford Origination Ltd
Chelmsford, Essex
and printed in Great Britain by
Anchor Brendon Ltd, Tiptree, Essex
for the publishers
B. T. Batsford Ltd
4 Fitzhardinge Street
London W1H 0AH

Contents

Introduction

Wood has played an important role in the history of mankind and has provided a pleasant and attractive medium for man to demonstrate his creative and artistic abilities. A particularly interesting aspect of this is toy-making, in which the tactile qualities of wood combine with the craftsman's ingenuity to produce a simple working model or toy that has an enduring charm for both children and adults.

Many of the toys featured in this book were well known to past generations, but with the advent of new materials and techniques they are now rapidly becoming things of the past. I have always been fascinated by working models in wood, an interest which stems from the pleasure I experienced as a small child when my father made me a working model of a crane in wood. Over the years, as I came across these traditional designs, I collected and recorded them so that future generations of children could have access to the pleasure and joy that these toys give. Because of the enduring nature of wood, the toys will often survive the rigours of play so that they can be handed down to the next generation and become treasured possessions within a family.

Note

The toys in this book were made using imperial measurements. For ease of reading, approximate metric equivalents are given in the text and diagrams. If, however, you wish to work in metric, you should follow the accurate conversions given in the table on page 87.

1. Tools

The tools mentioned in this section are those which you will need to make the toys described in the book. Although these tools would form the nucleus of a basic kit of tools, the list is by no means complete, as a kit will be dependent on the nature of the work tackled, and on personal preferences in the selection of tools acquired.

Care of tools

When buying tools it is always advisable to obtain the best quality that you can afford, as working with inferior tools will not give good results. Once you have acquired the tools, it is also necessary to keep them sharpened and well maintained as they are an investment which can last a lifetime, and if they are not kept in good condition they will deteriorate and produce poor-quality work.

Tools not in daily use should be lightly wiped with an oily rag after use to protect the steel surfaces from rust. Once the steel face of a tool has become pitted with rust, it will not be possible to form a keen cutting edge and the performance of the tool will be spoilt. The wooden parts of tools can be kept in good condition by an occasional light application of linseed oil. When tools are not being used it is a good idea to get into the habit of putting them away, because if they are left lying about on the bench top they can become damaged through contact with each other and may also be a source of danger, as a cluttered bench top leads to accidents. Tools are best stored in racks or cupboards with a place for each tool, to protect both the tools and the worker.

When using tools, remember that they are designed to do a specific task and they will perform that task just as easily on you as on the wood on which you are working, if you do not use them correctly. Always follow the safety precautions and do not stray from them, as it is at that moment that accidents are most likely to occur. A good craftsman is one who is careful, both in workmanship and safety.

Tenon saw

The tenon saw is also known as the back saw because of the steel or brass back fitted to the blade which keeps the blade in tension and gives it rigidity. This provides sufficient weight to cause the blade to cut when the saw is pushed through the wood. The saw is used for general bench work and for cutting joints. Normally it will have 12-14 teeth to 1 in (25 mm) and a comfortable length will be about 12 in (300 mm).

Care should be taken when using the saw that a twist does not develop; this can be seen by looking down the cutting edge. If the cutting edge is not straight, this may often be rectified by holding the saw in one hand and tapping the top of the steel or brass back with a hammer at the front end of the saw. Before using the saw, it helps to rub each side of the blade with candle wax, which reduces the effort of pushing the saw through the wood. When the saw becomes blunt, it will need to be sharpened to restore its cutting edge. Unless you are experienced in this, it is best left to an expert.

The blades of most saws will be made from the highest quality tool steel which is hardened and tempered so that it is both tough and elastic. The wooden handle should be made from good-quality knot-free beech.

Coping saw

The coping saw is intended for cutting curved shapes and consists of a spring steel frame with a wooden handle which will screw tight to provide tension for the blade. The blade is thin so that it will cut tight curves, but it is also hard and brittle, which causes it to snap easily if it is forced in use. However, the blades are relatively inexpensive and easy to replace. When putting the blade into the frame, check that the blade-holder pins in the frame are in line so that the blade is not twisted, and that the teeth of the blade point backwards towards the handle so that the blade cuts on the return stroke. By adjusting both the blade-holder pins so that they are at the same angle, the angle of the blade can be adjusted to suit the work. When the saw is not being used, it is good practice to unscrew the handle, as this will reduce the blade tension.

When using the coping saw, hold the handle with one hand only and do not try to cut the work quickly, as this usually results in the blade snapping. It is much better to use a slow and steady stroke. In fact, this advice holds true for all sawing operations. If you try to saw quickly the effectiveness of the saw is reduced because the teeth are not designed for a rapid feed, and you will also find it very tiring. Coping saw blades usually have 15-17 points to 1 in (25 mm) and are 6 in (150 mm) long. The frame of the saw will normally allow a depth of cut of 5 in (125 mm).

Fret saw

The fret saw is very similar to the coping saw both in appearance and use but it has, because of the shape of the frame, a greater depth of cut. The blade is finer, with 32 points to 1 in (25 mm), and is slightly shorter at 5 in (125 mm) in length. The depth of cut is greater, being 11 in (275 mm). The fret saw is generally used on thin material and because of the number of teeth it is a slow-cutting saw. Its advantage over the coping saw is its deeper throat which enables the blade to carry out work well inside the edge of a piece of wood.

Remember, when sawing, that a wide-bladed saw such as the tenon saw should be used for sawing straight lines, and narrow-bladed saws such as the coping saw or fret saw should only be used for cutting curved lines.

Junior hacksaw

The junior hacksaw has a sprung steel frame with a hardwood handle. It is used for general light work where a standard hacksaw would be too big or clumsy. The blades are flexible with 32 teeth to 1 in (25 mm) and are 6 in (150 mm) long. Tension is applied to the blade by screwing up the handle. The teeth of the blade should point to the front of the saw when fitted.

Bench hook

This is sometimes known as a sawing board, and it is used to steady work when sawing, often with one end gripped in a vice so that the bench hook is firmly held. It is particularly useful when wood is cut across the grain. The bench hook also protects the bench top from damage by the saw. A good-quality bench hook will be made from beech.

Try square

The try square consists of a tool-steel blade which is set at right angles to the stock. The stock of the try square is usually faced with a strip of brass to reduce wear. The blade is firmly secured in the stock by means of brass or mild steel rivets. Its chief uses are for testing external and internal right angles, and for marking out when a line is required at right angles to an edge. The tool should be handled carefully to avoid damaging the blade and knocking it out of square from the stock. Remember, when using the try square, that it will only draw lines at right angles to an edge if the stock is kept firmly in contact with the edge.

Marking knife

Marking knives are usually made of tool steel with a rosewood handle which is riveted onto the steel blade. The blade is ground to a bevelled skew and sharpened on the outside face, allowing the inside face to be kept tightly against the edge of the try square or steel rule. A marking knife is only used when the line is to be cut with either a saw or a chisel. If the line is not intended to be cut, a pencil should be used instead.

Marking gauge

The stock of the marking gauge acts as a fence and is locked onto the stem by means of a thumb screw which allows the stem to be adjusted to the desired measurement. In good-quality tools, the stock is faced with two brass strips to protect it against wear when in use. The hardened steel spur at the end of the stem scribes a line parallel to an edge either along the grain or on the end grain.

When using the marking gauge, hold it so that the spur is not at right angles vertically to the face of the wood, as this would tend to dig in, but rather hold the marking gauge so that the spur trails along at an acute angle. This will tend to prevent the spur following the grain of the wood. It is better to make two or three lighter scores with the gauge than to try to make one heavy score. The best marking gauges are usually made from beech and the thumb screw is made of boxwood.

Steel rule

The steel rule is an essential part of the tool kit for accurate marking out. It must be handled with care, as the measurements start immediately from the square end; this is so that it can be used for setting the marking gauge and measuring internal dimensions easily. It may also be used as a straight edge. Steel rules are normally made of stainless steel and can often be purchased with metric divisions on one edge and imperial on the other.

Centre punch

The centre punch is made from tempered and hardened tool steel. It is used for marking the position of the centre of holes to be drilled in metal. The centre punch is held in a vertical position and a light blow with a hammer is sufficient to make a mark in the metal. This mark will prevent the drill wandering when it is introduced to the work, and for accurate drilling of metal it is essential.

Hand drill

The hand drill is useful for drilling holes up to ¼ in (6 mm) diameter. The best hand drills have a double pinion drive which is stronger and gives a smoother action than the single pinion drive. The chuck is fitted with three jaws and is designed to grip round-shanked drills. The hand drill is a useful tool and is fairly accurate. Light oiling of working parts assists the smooth working of the hand drill.

Brace

The brace is a more rugged drill which is used for large, deep hole-boring. The best braces are those fitted with a ratchet, and these can be worked in a confined space. The chuck is fitted with two jaws and is designed to fit the square shank of the larger drills which are called bits. When in use the brace must be maintained square to the work so that a true hole will result. The working parts should be lightly oiled from time to time for ease of working and to reduce wear.

Twist drill

The throat of the woodworker's twist drill is specially designed to clear away the wood chips on both hard and soft wood when drilling at high speed. The sides of the twist drill are parallel, which improves their accuracy when in use. They are normally available in a range of sizes from ¹⁄₆₄ in (0.38 mm) to ½ in (12.5 mm). The twist drill is often used in conjunction with the hand drill, usually for drilling smaller holes.

Jenning's pattern auger bit

When larger holes are required a Jenning's pattern auger bit is used with the brace. The auger bit has a spiral point which draws the bit into the wood. The spur cutters sever the fibres of the wood and the router cutter removes the waste wood from the hole. This type of bit is used to bore deep holes with a reasonable degree of accuracy as the sides of the bit are parallel. These drills come in a range of sizes from 3⁄16 in (4.5 mm) to 1½ in (37.5 mm).

Bradawl

The bradawl is used for making holes in wood in preparation for small screws and nails. This reduces the danger of the screws or nails splitting the wood. The blade is similar in shape to a screwdriver and is made in cast steel. When it is used, the cutting edge should be placed at right angles to the fibres of the wood so that the fibres are cut and not just pushed to one side. Once it has penetrated the wood, the blade is then twisted. The handle of the bradawl is usually made from beech or ash and it should also be fitted with a ferrule to increase the strength of the tool.

Screwdrivers

There are many types of screwdriver, but the most commonly used is the cabinet screwdriver, the blade of which should be made from tempered alloy steel, which is necessary to withstand the pressure exerted on the blade when it is in use. To resist this force, the round blade is traditionally flattened towards the handle to form a tang. The oval-shaped beechwood handles are fitted with a steel ferrule to stop the handle splitting when in use. Where the new plastic handles are used, the blade is not flattened and a steel ferrule is not necessary.

Cabinet screwdrivers come in a range of sizes from 3 in (75 mm) to 10 in (250 mm). The tip of the screwdriver should be cross-ground and should fit the slot of the screw closely. If the blade is too narrow for the slot of the screw, the excessive leverage required from the screwdriver to drive the screw into the wood will tend to damage the head of the screw. If the blade is too wide, it will cause damage to the surrounding wood. If the tip of the screwdriver is not correctly ground, it will not grip the slot of the screw; it may then slip out and damage the head of the screw or the surrounding wood.

Woodworker's mallet

The woodworker's mallet is also sometimes called the joiner's mallet. Both the head and shaft of the mallet are made of beech, with the shaft entering the head through a tapered hole. The blow delivered by a mallet is duller than that of a hammer, and since the striking surface is larger, the resultant blow is distributed over a wider area. Mallets should always be used when working with chisels as they are less likely than hammers to damage the chisel handle; conversely, the mallet should not be used to strike metal objects as this will damage its faces. It is a good idea to apply a thin coat of linseed oil to the mallet frequently, as this will protect the wood and keep it in good condition. Mallets come in various sizes — choose one of a weight and size suitable for you.

Cross-pein hammer

The head of the hammer is made from tool steel and the face is hardened and tempered to resist wear. The pein is also hardened and tempered. The shaft of the hammer is usually made from ash or hickory. The cross-pein hammer is the most common general-purpose hammer for carpentry and joinery. The face is used mainly for driving nails into timber and the pein for starting small nails which may be held between the forefinger and thumb. These hammers come in a variety of sizes, and again it is a good idea to select one of the size and weight that suits you. Personally, I find the smaller sizes to be the most useful.

Nail punch

The heads of nails very often need to be sunk below the surface of the work as they are inclined to work out over a period of time and can be unsightly if left showing. The nail punch is used to drive the nail head below the surface of the wood. The hollowed point of the punch is placed on the nail head and the head of the punch is struck with a hammer. Nail punches are made from high-carbon steel hardened and tempered, with a centre section knurled to provide a grip for the fingers.

Plane

The body of the plane is a metal block with the sides and the sole machined. The blade and other parts are fitted into the body which is made from high-quality cast iron. The blade adjustments are easy to make and with the handle positioned low down on the body, the plane is fairly easy to control in use.

The plane is used for reducing the thickness and width of a piece of wood, for making it straight and also for smoothing it to a good finish. A plane is fitted with a cap iron which prevents the blade from chattering or vibrating, and gives a smoother finish. The blade is made from tool steel which is hardened and tempered. The jack plane is a good general-purpose plane for jointing and final smoothing. A useful size is 14 in (350 mm) with a blade 2 in (50 mm) wide. A piece of candle rubbed frequently on the sole of the plane will lubricate it and reduce the effort of using it considerably. After using the plane, place it on its side to avoid dulling the blade or damaging the work surface.

Rebate plane

The rebate plane has a cast-iron body and is used for cutting rebates along the edges of timber. It is fitted wth an adjustable depth stop and an adjustable fence.

The depth stop determines the depth of the rebate, and the fence determines the breadth of the rebate. The width of the blade is normally 1 in (25 mm). Before using the rebate plane on your work, test it on a scrap piece of wood to check that you have set the plane accurately.

Spokeshave

The stock of the spokeshave is made from cast iron and the blade from tool steel. The flat-bottom spokeshave is used for cutting a convex curve and the round-bottom spokeshave for cutting a concave curve. The spokeshave is used mainly for finishing curved surfaces to the desired contour. When using the spokeshave, always work from short to long grain on narrow sections of wood.

Chisels

The handles of chisels should be made from good quality hardwood such as box or beech. Plastic handles are now also obtainable, but I prefer the wooden handle as this tends to absorb any perspiration from the hand when the tool is being used. The blade of the chisel is made from high-carbon steel which is hardened and tempered. The cutting edge of the chisel has two distinct bevels. The first bevel is obtained by grinding the end of the chisel on the grindstone to an angle of 20-25°. This angle is called the grinding bevel. The second bevel is obtained when the ground chisel edge is sharpened on an oilstone to an angle of approximately 25-30°. This is called the sharpening bevel.

A useful chisel is the firmer chisel, available in a range of sizes from ¼ in (6 mm) to 1 in (25 mm). The blade of the firmer chisel is rectangular in section, which makes it fairly strong and useful for general work such as removing the waste wood from various joints; because of the strength of the blade the chisel will accept light blows from a woodworker's mallet. Great care should be taken when using the chisel as incorrect use will make it a potentially very dangerous tool.

Files

Files are useful for cleaning up shaped edges and particularly in places where the spokeshave would be awkward to use. The disadvantage of a file is that it does not give the crisp finish which would be obtained with an edge tool, as instead of cutting the wood it is inclined to wear it away. This can be overcome to a certain extent by finishing the work with glasspaper after the shaping has been acquired with the file.

The half-round file

The half-round file has a relatively smooth action when shaping wood. The rounded side is particularly useful for shaping hollow or concave curves, while the flat side is used for rounded or convex curves. This file comes in a variety of sizes and a useful size would be 10-12 in (250-300 mm). When filing, the teeth of the file will become clogged with the waste wood and it will then be necessary to use a file card to remove the waste material. This is done by moving the file card backwards and forwards across the file in line with the cut or teeth of the file.

G cramp

G cramps are invaluable for such jobs as gluing together small pieces of wood, holding pieces of wood together while marking out, and clamping work down to the bench top for chiselling, sawing or shaping. The frame of the G cramp is made from malleable cast iron and the size of the cramp is the distance between the two jaws when fully opened; this varies from 2 in (50 mm) to 12 in (300 mm). When using the G cramp, always put a piece of scrap wood between the work and the faces of the G cramp to prevent the surface of the work being marked or dented by the metal jaws of the G cramp.

2. Fixtures and Fittings

Nails

Nails are a quick and fairly effective means of joining wood to wood. They hold the wood together by the friction of the nail against the fibres of the wood, which means that the strength of the joint is limited. For a more permanent job it is better to use nails in combination with an adhesive.

Wire nails
Wire nails (figure 1) are normally used for general construction work where looks are not important. The nail has a fairly large head which is serrated in order to give the hammer grip when the head is hit. The neck is also serrated to increase its grip in the wood. The section of the nail is circular. It is available in sizes ranging from ¾ in (18 mm) to 6 in (150 mm).

Figure 1

Panel pins
The panel pin (figure 2) has a very fine shank and is used by cabinet-makers for fixing mouldings and other fine work. The nail is circular in section, and the head of the pin is small enough to allow it to be concealed by punching it with a nail punch below the surface of the wood. The size of panel pins ranges from ½ in (12.5 mm) to 2 in (50 mm).

Veneer pins
The veneer pin (figure 3) is similar in shape to the panel pin but it is much finer in section. It is normally used for temporarily holding veneers in position on the ground before they are taped, while the adhesive sets. The size of veneer pins ranges from ½ in (12.5 mm) to 2 in (50 mm).

Figure 3

Upholstery nails
The upholstery nail (figure 4) has a large dome-shaped head which is often plated with bronze or brass; it is used for attaching materials to a wooden base, as in upholstery. Upholstery nails are usually ½ in (12.5 mm) long.

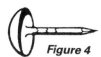

Figure 4

Screws

Wood screws are most commonly made from mild steel or brass. The shape of the head determines the type of screw and its use. The shank of the screw is pointed and is threaded for two-thirds of its length. It is

Figure 2

the thread of the screw which pulls the screw into the wood. Screws are used for fastening wood to wood and for fitting hardware to wood. The main advantage of screws in comparison with nails is their additional strength and ease of withdrawal.

Screws are defined by the length of the screw, the thickness of the shank or gauge, the material from which the screw is made and the type of head. They are normally available in sizes ranging from ⅜ in (9 mm) to 6 in (150 mm) and in a variety of gauges to suit the differing uses for a given length.

Countersunk screws

Countersunk screws (figure 5) are used for general woodwork when a flush finished surface is required. The head of the screw will normally lie slightly below the surface of the wood.

Figure 5

Round-head screws

The round-head screw (figure 6) is frequently used for securing external metal fittings to wood, and also where an ornamental finish is required, as the head is left raised above the surface.

Figure 6

Adhesives

A simple-to-use and efficient adhesive for interior work is polyvinyl acetate adhesive, more commonly shortened to PVA. The adhesive is white in colour and is the consistency of thick cream. It is supplied ready to use in a handy container. PVA does not stain the wood and has a very long shelf life. Its bonding qualities are very good and it will usually set in two to three hours at normal room temperature. It is most efficient when the glued joint is clamped. Its gap-filling qualities are fair, but its water resistance is poor. As it is soluble in water it does have the advantage that if it is spilt on clothes it can be removed by soaking.

3. Finishing

It is always most important to finish your work to a high standard. This will make the piece pleasant to touch and visually appealing, as well as protecting it and keeping it in good condition. A piece of work carefully made and well finished is a most satisfying conclusion to a project.

Once the work has been cut to shape and fitted, then it may be necessary to use a filler to fill holes made by nails or screws, or to repair damage to the wood caused by splintering or other blemishes. Splintering most frequently occurs when sawing or filing plywood, and is particularly unsightly if not filled. Wood fillers of different qualities can be obtained from many shops and they are available in a variety of different colours to be used under all decorative finishes.

Before applying a filler, make sure that you have read the instructions and that the area to be filled is dry and free of dust. Blow away the dust or use a brush to do this. Then apply the filler with a knife or a chisel and press it firmly into the hole, ensuring that it is well filled and left slightly proud. Once the filler is dry, it is then ready for glasspapering to remove the surplus. If the wood is to be finished with a natural finish, take care that you match the filler to the colour of the wood. This is not so important if the work is to be painted.

The piece of work must be cleaned up thoroughly in preparation for whatever finish you may choose, and this is done with an abrasive paper called glasspaper. Glasspaper is made from finely crushed glass, which is sprinkled over stiff paper previously coated with glue. Fine sand was originally used for this purpose

which is why glasspaper is still often incorrectly called sandpaper.

During the crushing process, the particles of glass are graded and the sizes are denoted by numbers which are printed on the sheets of glasspaper. The very finest are known as flourpaper. For general work I would choose an M2, which is a medium-rough grade of glasspaper and is particularly useful if minor shaping is involved; as it is quite a coarse paper it will remove small amounts of surplus wood fairly quickly. However, it does leave a rough finish to your work and if minor shaping is not necessary, it is best to use the F2 grade which is much finer and will give your work a smoother and more pleasing finish. If it is necessary to use the M2 grade, you must follow it with the F2 grade; then, for a really smooth finish, I always finish by using a flourpaper.

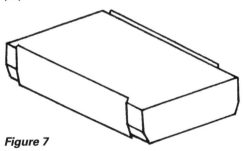

Figure 7

A piece of glasspaper of suitable size is cut from the sheet; for economy, you will be able to get six pieces from a standard-sized sheet. The piece of glasspaper is wrapped around a cork rubber as shown in figure 7. The advantage of using a cork rubber when glasspapering is that the pressure is more evenly distributed, and a flat surface more easily obtained. The use of the cork rubber also helps to preserve corners, which is an important factor if the finished article is to have clean, crisp lines. The cork rubber with the glasspaper wrapped around it is held as shown in figure 8 and a moderate pressure is applied, as the cork rubber is moved to and fro along the length of the surface of the wood in line with the grain. When you are doing this, make sure that the whole surface is glasspapered.

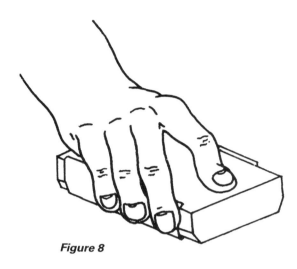

Figure 8

When cleaning up curved edges or corners, it is sometimes more efficient to dispense with the cork rubber and to glasspaper by hand, folding the glasspaper in half so that the upper abrasive face of the glasspaper gives the fingers a grip.

The action of glasspaper is different to that of a cutting tool, which gives a clean finish. Glasspaper is an abrasive and must always be used along the grain of the wood as it removes the wood by scratching. If you use glasspaper across the grain of the wood, the scratches will be much more pronounced and will spoil your finish.

It must be remembered that glasspapering is essentially a finishing-off process.

It is not intended to remove deep grooves or tool marks, so the surface must always be made as smooth as possible with a plane or smooth file before glasspaper is used.

If necessary, fill any holes on the surface of your work and carefully rub down through the grades from rough to medium and to fine, so that the piece will be ready to have a finish applied to it. Toys look their best if they are finished in bright colours or with a natural finish which reveals the grain of the wood. A natural finish is attractive if used with a hardwood. For some models a mixture of both natural and bright colours is particularly effective.

Paint

Many paints contain toxic materials which are dangerous if they are introduced into the body. This is a particular hazard where children are concerned, as they will often suck or chew a toy. So always check when you are buying paints for toys that they are non-toxic and safe to use for children's toys. Remember that you must buy primer, undercoat and topcoat that are all non-toxic and do not be tempted to use other primers and undercoats that you may have in stock. There is a wide range of colours available which, when used on a softwood, can add excitement and impact to your model.

If the toys are to be used outside it is advisable to give the work a coat of priming paint first. When this is dry, lightly flat down the work with a piece of used flourpaper before applying a coat of undercoat. This will seal the wood and give a good base for the gloss coat. For a really good finish apply two topcoats to your work, once again flatting down with used flourpaper between coats. This will give your work a really durable and high-gloss finish. If the toy is to be used indoors only, you may dispense with the primer. If you want to paint patterns on your work, this may be done by using masking tape once the gloss coat has thoroughly dried.

Varnish

Polyurethane varnish will keep and enhance the natural look of your wood while at the same time protecting it. Check that the varnish you use is non-toxic and is safe to use on children's toys. Normally, varnish can be bought with three types of finish — gloss, matt and satin — all of which look especially good when used on a hardwood. For a good finish apply three or four thin coats of varnish, allowing adequate time between coats for drying, and also flatting down between coats with used flourpaper.

The golden rule for a good finish with paint or varnish is to allow plenty of time for each coat to dry and harden before flatting down and applying the next coat. Try to make sure that your work and painting area is as free from dust as possible and that your paintbrushes are clean and of a good quality. Avoid putting on thick coats of paint or varnish, as they will not dry well and will look like treacle. Brush out the paint carefully and, if possible, in line with the grain. To keep your brushes clean you will need the recommended thinners for the paint or varnish which you are using. Always read the instructions carefully before you start, and follow them. A high-quality finish is worth all the time and effort spent on good craftsmanship and careful preparation.

4. Hook Trick

Materials

Body and finger grip: 1 off ⅝ × ⅝ × 4¼ in
  (15 × 15 × 106 mm) hardwood
Plunger: 1 off 4 × ¼ in (100 × 6 mm) beech
  dowel
1 elastic band
adhesive
varnish

Tools

tenon saw
¼ in (6 mm) drill
hand drill
bench hook
half-round file
cork rubber
glasspaper

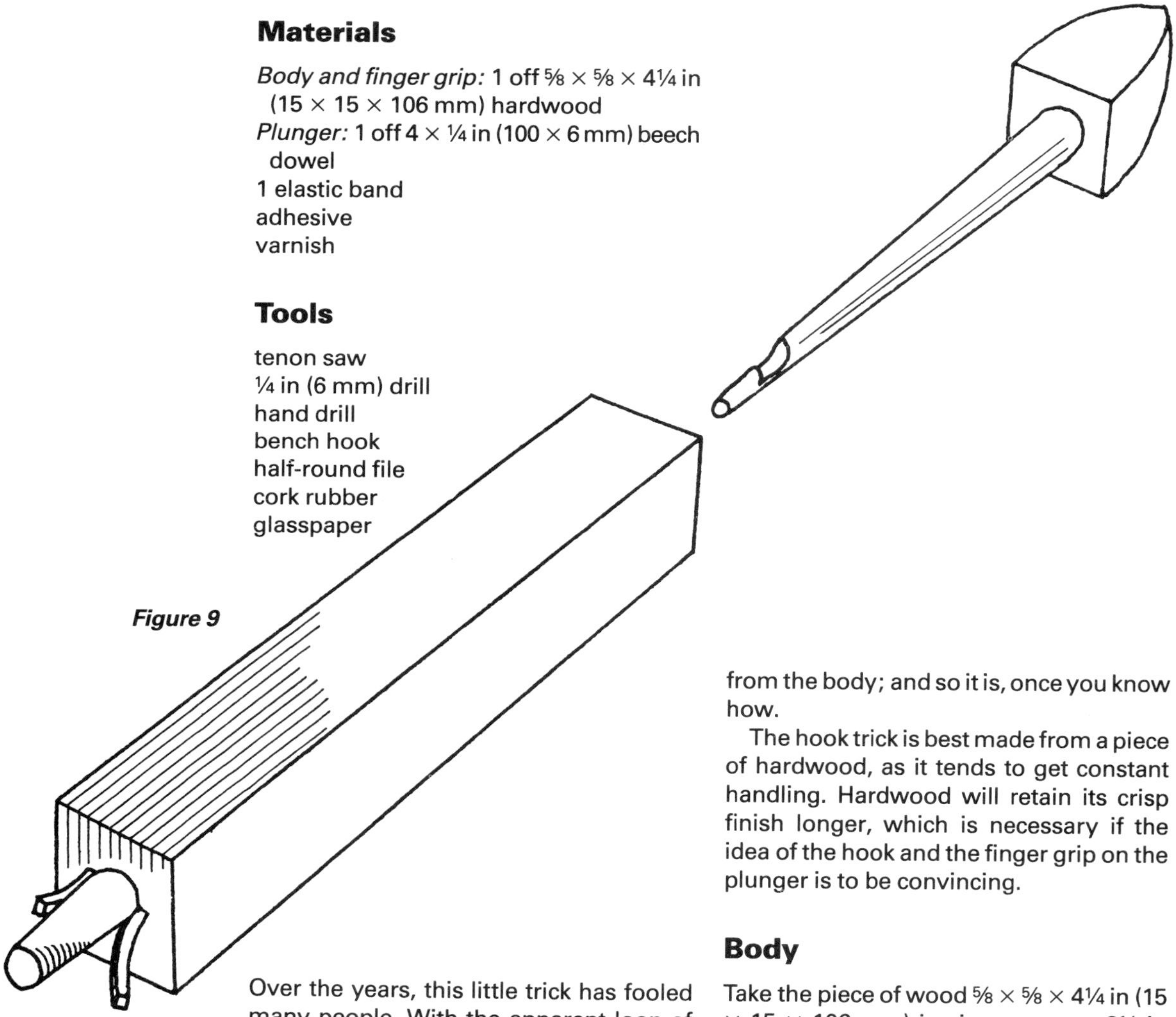

Figure 9

Over the years, this little trick has fooled many people. With the apparent loop of elastic band in one end of the body, it would seem to be the easiest thing in the world to catch it on the hook of the plunger, so that the plunger springs back out of your grip when you try to remove it from the body; and so it is, once you know how.

The hook trick is best made from a piece of hardwood, as it tends to get constant handling. Hardwood will retain its crisp finish longer, which is necessary if the idea of the hook and the finger grip on the plunger is to be convincing.

Body

Take the piece of wood ⅝ × ⅝ × 4¼ in (15 × 15 × 106 mm) in size, measure 3½ in (87.5 mm) and saw to size using a tenon saw and bench hook. Mark each end of the long piece with diagonal lines to find the centre, in preparation for drilling. This piece is the body.

Now mount this vertically in a vice and carefully drill a ¼ in (6mm) diameter hole right through the centre (figure 10). If your drill is not long enough to go right through, turn the work round in the vice and drill from the other end, so that the holes meet accurately in the centre.

Next, cut a piece of ¼ in (6 mm) dowel 1 in (25 mm) long. Take two short pieces of an elastic band, and with the dowel push them into the hole in the body for about ½ in (12.5 mm), making sure that the pieces of elastic band are clearly visible (figure 11). If the dowel and elastic bands do not form a tight fit, secure them in position with adhesive.

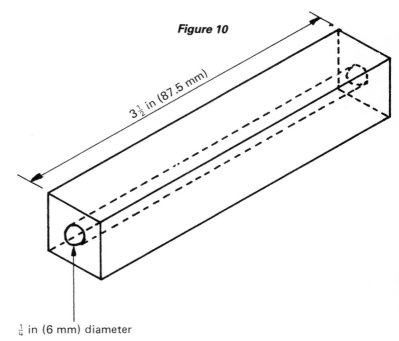

Figure 10

3½ in (87.5 mm)

¼ in (6 mm) diameter

Figure 11

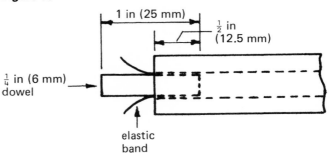

1 in (25 mm)

½ in (12.5 mm)

¼ in (6 mm) dowel

elastic band

Plunger and finger grip

Use the remaining piece of ⅝ × ⅝ × ¾ in (15 × 15 × 18 mm) hardwood to make the finger grip of the plunger. On one end draw diagonals, and using a ¼ in (6 mm) diameter drill, drill in ⅜ in (9 mm). Check that the remaining piece of ¼ × 3 in (6 × 75 mm) dowel fits into it snugly to form the plunger (figure 12).

Remove the piece of dowel and using a half-round file, taper the dowel along its length, so that it will fit easily into the body. Cut a hook ¼ in (6 mm) from the

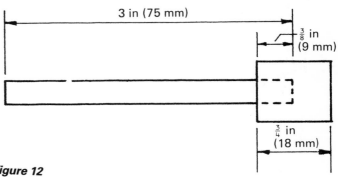

3 in (75 mm)

⅜ in (9 mm)

¾ in (18 mm)

Figure 12

19

end, using the edge of a half-round file. Shape the finger grip on all four faces using a half-round file and glasspaper (figure 13). When the plunger and finger grip are finished, spread a thin smear of glue in the hole of the finger grip and push home the plunger.

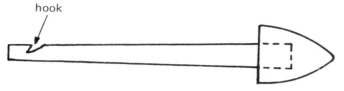
hook

Figure 13

Finishing

Finish the hook trick by smoothing down with glasspaper and applying two or three coats of varnish.

Solution

Place the plunger into the body and in front of your audience; let them think that there is a special position to line up the finger grip with the body. This can be made more convincing if a combination of dots is put on the sides of the body and finger grip, so that the observer will be led to believe that in some way, this is essential to the catching of the elastic band on the hook. The dots can be made either with paint of different colours or with a ball-point pen.

When the audience have seen you line up the dots, let them watch you carefully rotate the finger grip slightly from left to right, as if you are catching the elastic band on the hook. Then slowly remove the plunger from the body to about half its length; now tightly squeeze the finger grip between your finger and thumb, so that the plunger shoots back into the body with a loud click, making it appear that this has occurred through the power of the elastic band.

5. Bead Puzzle

Materials

Body: 1 off 6 × 1 × 1 in (150 × 25 × 25 mm) hardwood or softwood.
Beads: 2 off ⅝ in (15 mm) diameter beads or 2 off ⅝ × ⅝ in (15 × 15 mm) hardwood or softwood to be painted in contrasting colours
28 in (700 mm) of ⅛ in (3 mm) nylon cord
enamel paint
varnish

Tools

tenon saw
hand drill
³⁄₁₆ in (4.5 mm) drill
⅜ in (9 mm) drill
cork rubber
glasspaper

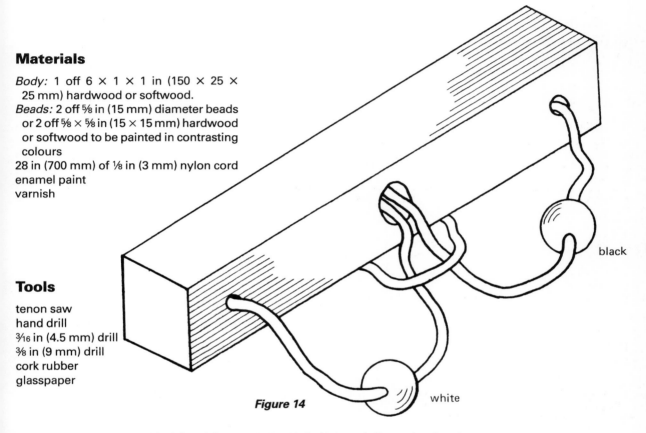

black

white

Figure 14

How can you move the black bead from one loop along the string to join the white bead in the other loop without untying the knots? This little puzzle is very simple to make and to solve once you know how, but to the uninitiated it will appear to be an almost impossible task.

To make the puzzle you will need a piece of wood 6 × 1 × 1 in (150 × 25 × 25 mm). Choose hardwood in preference, but if this is not available, a piece of softwood will be adequate. Mark out the wood as shown in figure 15, and drill the centre hole ⅜ in (9 mm) and the two end

holes ³⁄₁₆ in (4.5 mm). If your local craft or model shop does not stock ⅝ in (15 mm) diameter beads, take another piece of wood ⅝ × ⅝ in (15 × 15 mm) square and cut off two pieces ⅝ in (15 mm) long to make two cubes instead of the beads (figure 16). You will need to drill a hole through the centre of each cube ³⁄₁₆ in (4.5 mm) in diameter, and if you lightly round the corners of the cubes they will pass through the loops of the cord more easily when you are working the puzzle. Before assembling the puzzle, give the wood a smooth finish with glasspaper

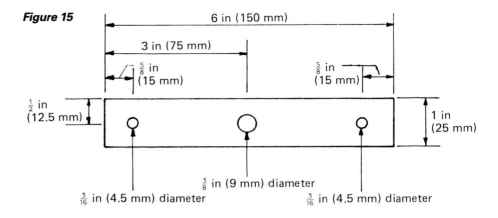

Figure 15

6 in (150 mm)

3 in (75 mm)

$\frac{5}{8}$ in (15 mm)

$\frac{5}{8}$ in (15 mm)

$\frac{1}{2}$ in (12.5 mm)

1 in (25 mm)

$\frac{3}{8}$ in (9 mm) diameter

$\frac{3}{16}$ in (4.5 mm) diameter

$\frac{3}{16}$ in (4.5 mm) diameter

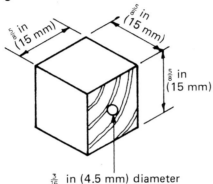

Figure 16

$\frac{5}{8}$ in (15 mm)

$\frac{5}{8}$ in (15 mm)

$\frac{5}{8}$ in (15 mm)

$\frac{3}{16}$ in (4.5 mm) diameter

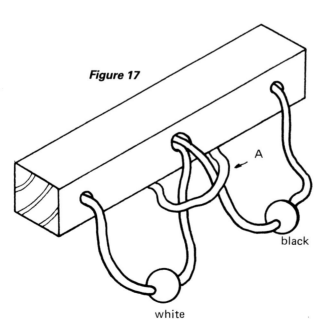

Figure 17

A

black

white

and apply two or three coats of varnish. Paint the beads in contrasting colours using enamel paint.

To assemble the puzzle, take a 28 in (700 mm) piece of ⅛ in (3 mm) nylon cord, and thread it through the holes as shown, not forgetting to thread the beads in the appropriate positions as you go. Firmly knot each end, and you are now ready to solve the puzzle. If you finally have to admit defeat, look at the solution, but don't show the answer to your friends.

Solution

Hold the puzzle in the position shown in figure 17, so that the knots are at the back. Take the black bead and pass it under the loop at A and hold it by the bar as in figure 18. Take hold of the two pieces of cord at B as they come through the centre hole and pull them towards you so that the double loop comes through the hole as in figure 19. The bead which is still on the right is now passed through the two loops at C and the double loop is pulled back through the centre hole. The bead is now passed through the single remaining loop so that it joins its partner in the loop on the other side (figure 20). By reversing this process, the two beads can be separated back to their original positions.

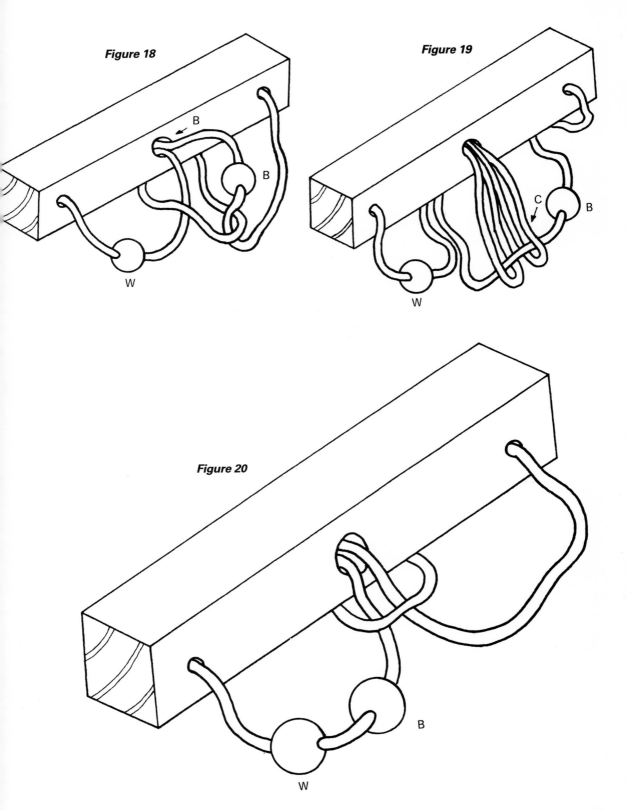

Figure 18

Figure 19

Figure 20

23

6. Magic Propeller

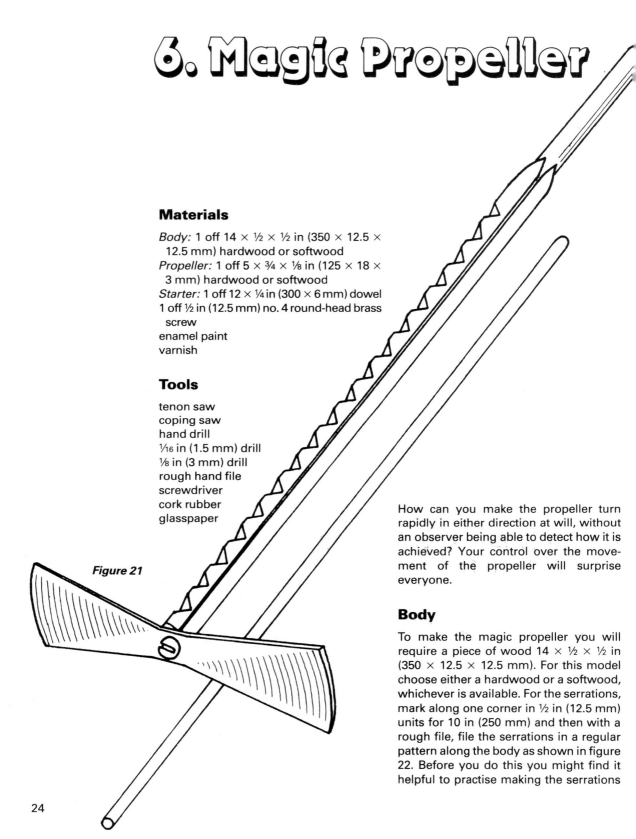

Materials

Body: 1 off 14 × ½ × ½ in (350 × 12.5 ×
   12.5 mm) hardwood or softwood
Propeller: 1 off 5 × ¾ × ⅛ in (125 × 18 ×
   3 mm) hardwood or softwood
Starter: 1 off 12 × ¼ in (300 × 6 mm) dowel
1 off ½ in (12.5 mm) no. 4 round-head brass
   screw
enamel paint
varnish

Tools

tenon saw
coping saw
hand drill
¹⁄₁₆ in (1.5 mm) drill
⅛ in (3 mm) drill
rough hand file
screwdriver
cork rubber
glasspaper

Figure 21

How can you make the propeller turn
rapidly in either direction at will, without
an observer being able to detect how it is
achieved? Your control over the movement of the propeller will surprise
everyone.

Body

To make the magic propeller you will
require a piece of wood 14 × ½ × ½ in
(350 × 12.5 × 12.5 mm). For this model
choose either a hardwood or a softwood,
whichever is available. For the serrations,
mark along one corner in ½ in (12.5 mm)
units for 10 in (250 mm) and then with a
rough file, file the serrations in a regular
pattern along the body as shown in figure
22. Before you do this you might find it
helpful to practise making the serrations

24

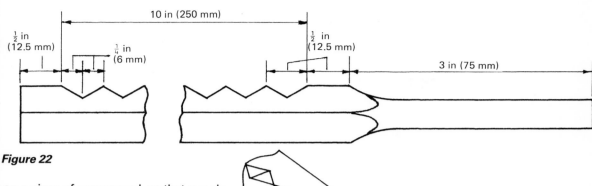

Figure 22

on a piece of scrap wood, so that you do not spoil your chosen piece.

For the handle of the body, measure 3 in (75 mm) along from the opposite end and with your file, round off the corners to give a smooth shape (figure 23). Now glasspaper the body and slightly round the corners to give a good finish.

Propeller

To make the propeller you will require a piece of wood 5 × ¾ × ⅛ in (125 × 18 × 3 mm). Mark out the propeller as shown in figure 24. First find the centre by drawing diagonals from corner to corner, then fol-

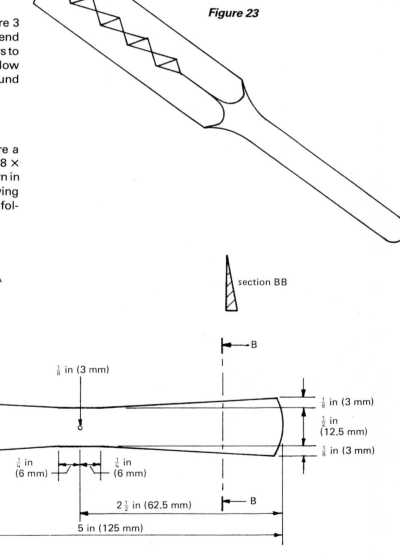

Figure 23

Figure 24

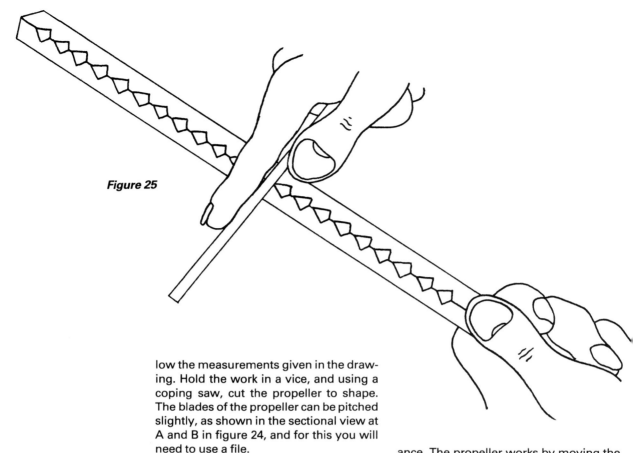

Figure 25

low the measurements given in the drawing. Hold the work in a vice, and using a coping saw, cut the propeller to shape. The blades of the propeller can be pitched slightly, as shown in the sectional view at A and B in figure 24, and for this you will need to use a file.

Drill the centre of the propeller with a ⅛ in (3 mm) drill then glasspaper the propeller to a satisfying and smooth finish. Before assembling the model, drill a small hole 1⁄16 in (1.5 mm) in diameter and ⅜ in (9 mm) deep in the centre of the end of the body, and screw the propeller on using a ½ in (12.5 mm) no. 4 round-head brass screw. For best results the screw should fit as closely as possible to the propeller whilst at the same time allowing it to rotate freely.

Starter

You will now need a 12 in (300 mm) piece of dowel ¼ in (6 mm) in diameter for driving the propeller. Clean up the model using glasspaper until a good finish is obtained, and then give it two or three coats of varnish. Painting the propeller with bright colours in the form of a decorative pattern improves the appear-

ance. The propeller works by moving the starting rod backwards and forwards along the serrations of the body. If you cannot make the propeller rotate in both directions read on.

Solution

Hold the starting rod with the index finger and thumb in position as shown in figure 25, so that the thumb is touching the side of the body. When the rod is moved backwards and forwards with the thumb in this position, the propeller will rotate anticlockwise.

To make the propeller rotate in a clockwise direction, move the rod over fractionally so that the index finger is now touching the other side when the rod is moved backwards and forwards as in figure 26. With a little practice, you will soon be able to do this without a casual observer noticing any change in the posi-

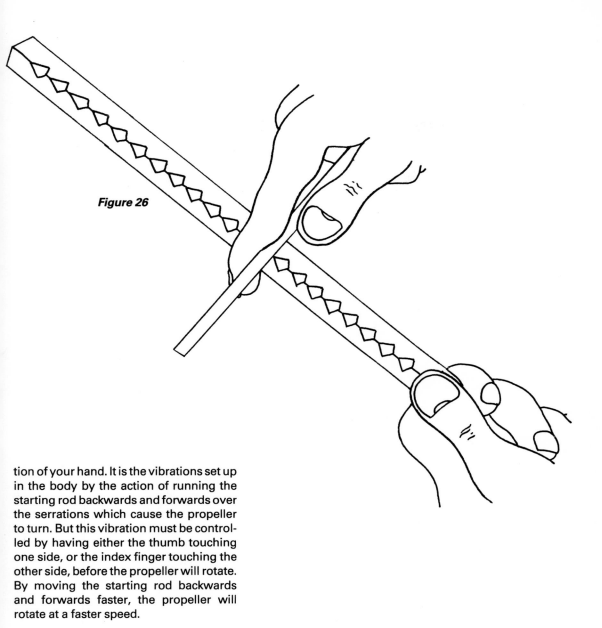

Figure 26

tion of your hand. It is the vibrations set up in the body by the action of running the starting rod backwards and forwards over the serrations which cause the propeller to turn. But this vibration must be controlled by having either the thumb touching one side, or the index finger touching the other side, before the propeller will rotate. By moving the starting rod backwards and forwards faster, the propeller will rotate at a faster speed.

7. Curler

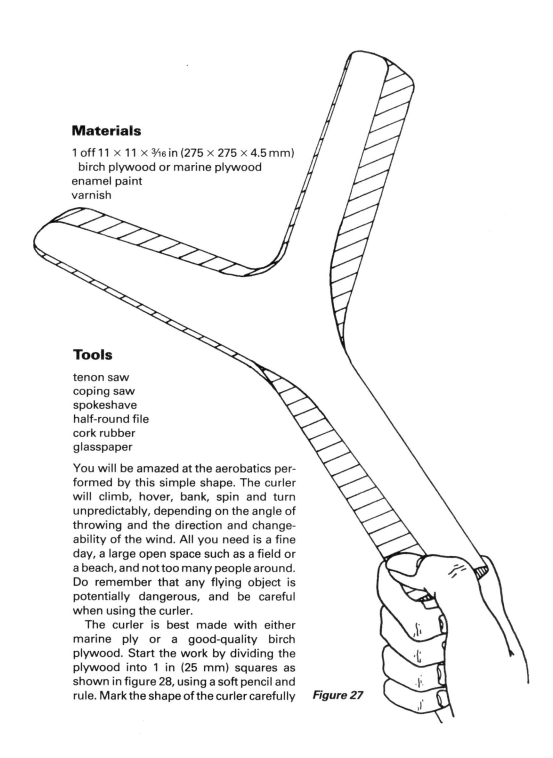

Materials

1 off 11 × 11 × 3/16 in (275 × 275 × 4.5 mm)
  birch plywood or marine plywood
enamel paint
varnish

Tools

tenon saw
coping saw
spokeshave
half-round file
cork rubber
glasspaper

You will be amazed at the aerobatics performed by this simple shape. The curler will climb, hover, bank, spin and turn unpredictably, depending on the angle of throwing and the direction and changeability of the wind. All you need is a fine day, a large open space such as a field or a beach, and not too many people around. Do remember that any flying object is potentially dangerous, and be careful when using the curler.

The curler is best made with either marine ply or a good-quality birch plywood. Start the work by dividing the plywood into 1 in (25 mm) squares as shown in figure 28, using a soft pencil and rule. Mark the shape of the curler carefully

Figure 27

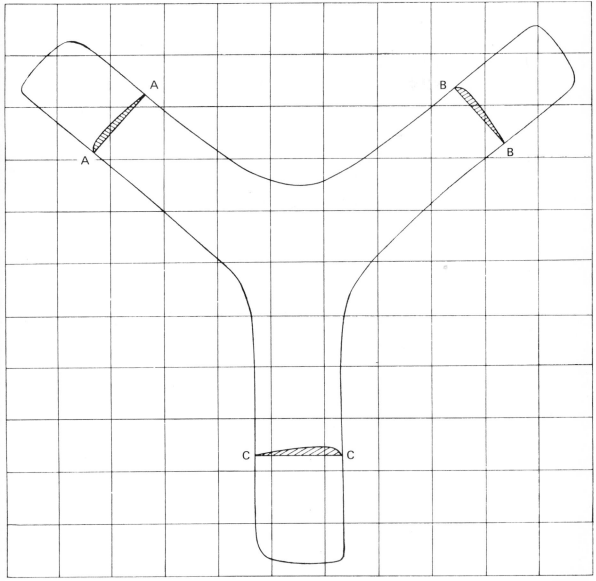

Figure 28   1 in (25 mm) squares

onto the plywood. Before cutting, check that the shape is correct and then use a tenon saw to cut the straight lines and a coping saw to cut the curved lines. For this you may find it useful to support the plywood in a vice while sawing. Adjust any irregularities in your sawing with a half-round file and glasspaper.

In the drawing (figure 28) you will notice that on each arm of the curler there is a sectional view — A, B and C — and in order for your curler to fly well, you must cut the blades as carefully as possible to the shape shown in the sectional view. Only the upper surface of the curler is shaped; the underside is left perfectly flat.

Use a finely adjusted spokeshave or half-round file to acquire the required shape. Note the similarity of shape between the curler and an aeroplane wing. This curler is designed for a right-handed person. If you are left-handed, shape the sections the reverse way round.

Using a medium-grade glasspaper and cork rubber, finish the curler to an accurate and smooth shape. Care at this stage is essential for a good performance. Give a final finish to the curler with two or three coats of varnish and decorate as you like with a brightly coloured pattern which will help to enhance its visual appeal when flying.

Using the curler

When you are using your curler for the first time, choose a still day or one with only a light wind. Hold the curler vertically by one of its arms between the finger and thumb of your right hand as shown in figure 27. Launch the curler from shoulder height by giving it a good throw horizontally, flicking your wrist just before you release it. This will make the curler spin, which is essential for it to begin its flight. If there is a light breeze, you will find it more spectacular if you launch it into the wind.

8. Boomerang

Materials

1 off 12 × 12 × ¼ in (300 × 300 × 6 mm)
  birch plywood or marine plywood
enamel paint
varnish

Tools

tenon saw   half-round file
coping saw   cork rubber
spokeshave   glasspaper

The boomerang is the weapon of the Australian Aborigines. They make two types — one which returns to the thrower, and one that is used as a weapon to inflict injury when hunting. The returning boomerang can be a plaything, but it is also used for training men to dodge weapons when hunting birds. Figure 29 shows the returning boomerang, and this is the one for which instructions are given. Once the technique for throwing has been mastered, you can enjoy it by yourself without involving others. Indeed, you should remember, when using your boomerang, that it is a potential weapon and must not be thrown when other people are around. This model takes very little time and material to make and is an interesting introduction to simple aerodynamics.

The basic proportions of the boomerang are a thickness of approximately one-sixth of its width, and a width of about one-twelfth of the total length. The top of the boomerang is convex, and the underside is more or less flat; provided that these proportions are maintained, the size of the boomerang can be increased or decreased accordingly. It is possible to make a returning boomerang to turn either to the left or to the right, and the model shown in figure 29 is designed to turn to the left, which is suitable for a right-handed person. If you are left-handed, then a right-handed model will be required and you should make a mirror-image copy.

To make a boomerang with 12 in (300 mm) arms, you will require a piece of good-quality ¼ in (6 mm) ply such as a birch plywood; the more expensive

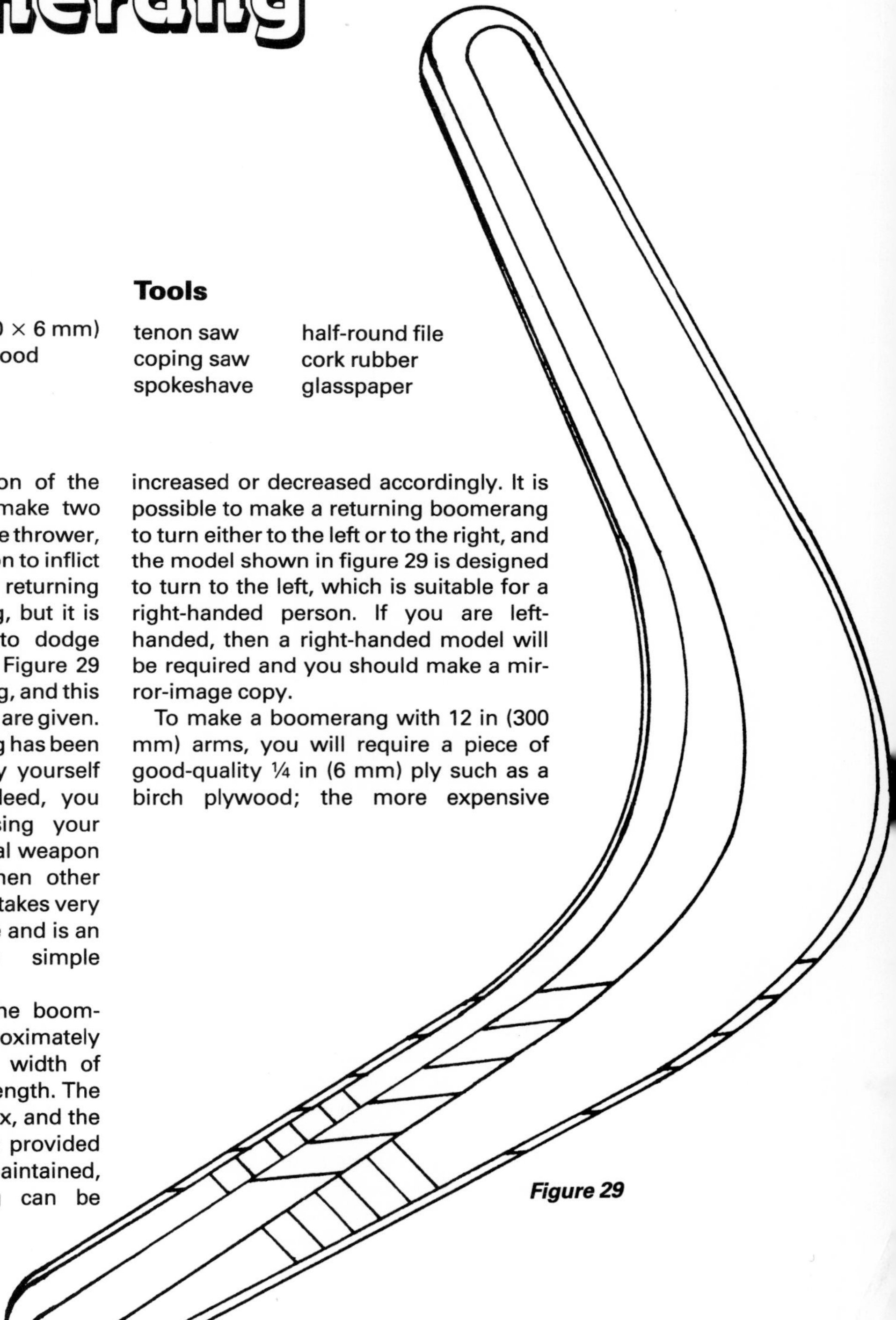

Figure 29

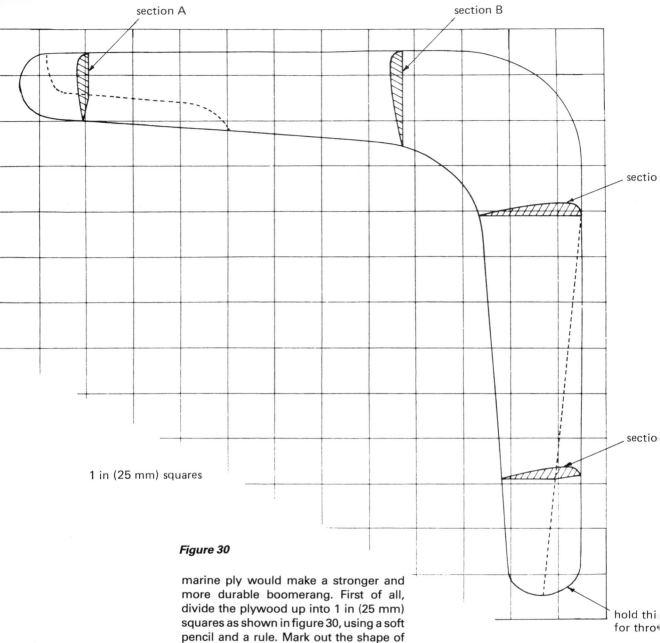

section A

section B

sectio

sectio

1 in (25 mm) squares

hold thi
for thro

Figure 30

marine ply would make a stronger and more durable boomerang. First of all, divide the plywood up into 1 in (25 mm) squares as shown in figure 30, using a soft pencil and a rule. Mark out the shape of the boomerang carefully onto the work. Once you are satisfied that your shape is correct, cut it out, using a tenon saw to cut the straight lines and a coping saw to cut the curved lines.

Figure 30 shows the four sections of the boomerang — A, B, C and D — and you should shape the sections as shown. The heavy line in the sectional view shows the underside of the boomerang. Shape the top of the boomerang by using a

spokeshave or half-round file to give the curve. The dotted lines show where the underside of the boomerang is chamfered at section A and section D. Once again, use the spokeshave or half-round file.

Using a medium-grade glasspaper, try to finish the boomerang as accurately as possible to the given sections; the final shaping of the chamfers at section A and

32

section D may require slight alteration after your test flight. If these chamfers are increased, it will cause the boomerang to make a sharper return. Once you are satisfied with the flight of your boomerang, glasspaper it down to a fine finish. It will look very attractive if it is decorated with brightly coloured motifs and then finished with two or three coats of varnish.

Using the boomerang

The boomerang performs best in fairly light wind. Hold the boomerang between finger and thumb (figure 31) and stand so that any wind is blowing on your left cheek. Throw the boomerang forwards and slightly upwards into the wind, making sure that as it leaves your hand it is spinning as much as possible. Just before release, flick your wrist to give added impetus to the flight. When you are throwing the boomerang correctly it should travel forwards for about 15-25 yards before it banks and climbs to the left and then returns in an arc to you. The return is caused by the skew of the boomerang combined with its spinning motion. Air pressure is created on the chamfers of the boomerang as they revolve, which causes it to turn in flight; this is why the shaping of these chamfers at section A and section D (figure 30) must be carried out as carefully as possible.

Figure 31

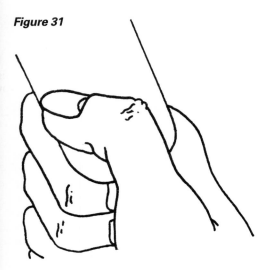

9. Sports Rattle

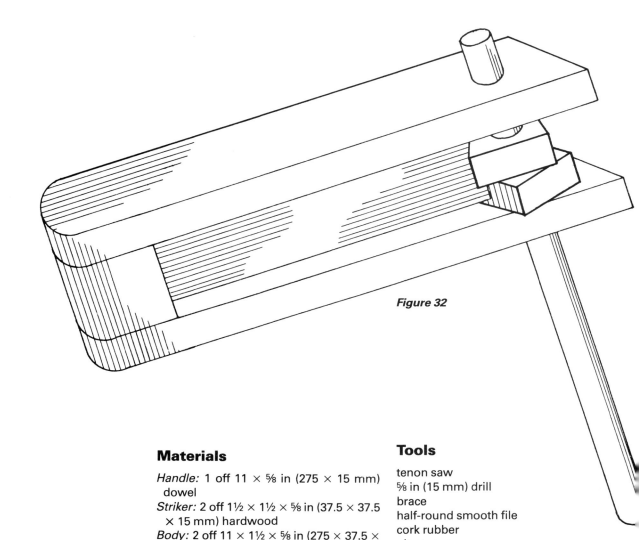

Figure 32

Materials

Handle: 1 off 11 × ⅝ in (275 × 15 mm) dowel

Striker: 2 off 1½ × 1½ × ⅝ in (37.5 × 37.5 × 15 mm) hardwood

Body: 2 off 11 × 1½ × ⅝ in (275 × 37.5 × 15 mm) hardwood

2 off 1¾ × 1½ × ⅝ in (43 × 37.5 × 15 mm) hardwood

Sound plate: 1 off 9 × 1⅜ × ³⁄₁₆ in (225 × 34 × 4.5 mm) birch plywood

8 off 1 in (25 mm) no. 6 countersunk brass screws

adhesive

enamel paint or varnish

Tools

tenon saw

⅝ in (15 mm) drill

brace

half-round smooth file

cork rubber

glasspaper

This is a model for the person who likes to be noticed. A few twists of the rattle are guaranteed to get you instant attention. It is amazing that such a simple device made from wood has such a loud noise output. It is great fun if you are the person using it, but not always so good if you are the person listening to it. However, when you are following your team, they will know you are right there, supporting them and spurring them on. Apart from the sporting application, the rattle will act as a most efficient deterrent in the garden for scaring birds away from the fruit trees and crops.

Handle

For the handle of the rattle you will need a piece of dowel 11 in (275 mm) long and ⅝ in (15 mm) in diameter. For the strikers you will need two pieces of hardwood 1½ × 1½ × ⅝ in (37.5 × 37.5 × 15 mm). Draw diagonals across the faces of the strikers from corner to corner to find the centres and then drill a hole in each of the strikers ⅝ in (15 mm) in diameter. Glue the strikers in position 1½ in (37.5 mm) down from the top of the handle (figure 33).

Body

For the body of the rattle you will need two pieces of hardwood 11 × 1½ × ⅝ in (275 × 37.5 × 15 mm) and two pieces of hardwood 1¾ × 1½ × ⅝ in (43 × 37.5 × 15 mm). Mark out the two 11 in (275 mm) pieces as shown in figure 34 and drill a hole ⅝ in (15 mm) in diameter in each piece. The handle will fit into these holes and should be able to rotate freely; it will therefore be necessary to enlarge slightly the holes with glasspaper wrapped around a piece of ½ in (12.5 mm) dowel until a suitable fit is obtained.

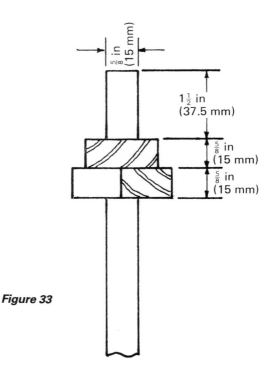

Figure 33

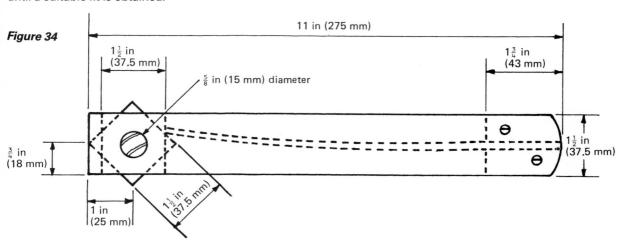

Figure 34

35

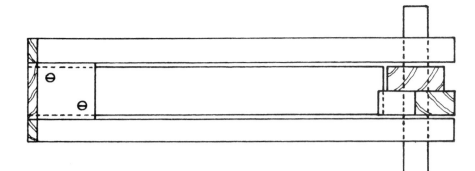

The sound plate

Figure 35

For the sound plate you will need a piece of plywood 9 × 1⅜ × ³⁄₁₆ in (225 × 34 × 4.5 mm) and this is held in position with the two pieces of hardwood 1¾ × 1½ × ⅝ in (43 × 37.5 × 15 mm) (figures 34, 35). It is essential that the plywood sound plate fits comfortably into the angle of the strikers when the work is finally assembled, as shown in figure 34. Drill and countersink the pieces as shown in figures 34 and 35 in preparation for screwing the work together. First of all screw the 1¾ × 1½ × ⅝ in (43 × 37.5 × 15 mm) pieces into position onto the sound plate using four 1 in (25 mm) no. 6 countersunk brass screws. Then assemble the complete rattle with the handle in position, and finally screw into place the top and bottom, again using your 1 in (25 mm) no. 6 countersunk brass screws. Lightly round the end of the rattle using a half-round smooth file as shown in figure 34.

Finishing

Dismantle the rattle and clean up with glasspaper ready for finishing. You can either finish with varnish, or if you like, the rattle can be painted to suit the colours of the team you support. When you are satisfied with this, all that is left to do is to reassemble the rattle, and it is ready for use.

10. Secret Money Box

Materials

Sides and ends: 1 off 24 × 3 × ⅝ in (600 × 75 × 15 mm) softwood or hardwood
Base: 1 off 7 × 3¼ × ⅝ in (175 × 81 × 15 mm) softwood or hardwood
Top: 1 off 8 × 4½ × ¼ in (200 × 112.5 × 6 mm) plywood
Locking bar: 1 off 3¾ × ½ in (93 × 12.5 mm) dowel
Pivoting pins: 2 off 1 × ⅛ in (25 × 3 mm) steel rods
1 off ½ in (12·5 mm) Terry clip
1 off ½ in (12·5 mm) no. 4 round-head brass screw
panel pins
adhesive
enamel paint
varnish

Tools

try square
tenon saw
hand drill
⅛ in (3 mm) drill
½ in (12·5 mm) drill
small file
hammer
nail punch

jack plane
bradawl
screwdriver
cork rubber
glasspaper
cramps
filler

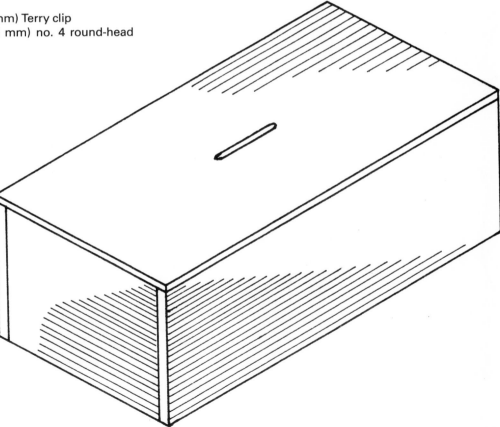

Figure 36

37

24 in (600 mm)

| 4 in (100 mm) | 8 in (200 mm) | 4 in (100 mm) | 8 in (200 mm) |

3 in (75 mm)

Figure 37

Boxes are always fascinating to make, especially a money box, which tends to bring out the Scrooge in everyone. This little box with its secret opening makes saving a pleasure, and is an ideal way of giving youngsters an incentive to save.

Sides and ends

The box illustrated is made from pine which is a softwood, but of course a hardwood, if available, would be just as suitable. To make the sides of the box you will require a piece of wood 24 × 3 × ⅝ in (600 × 75 × 15 mm). Mark it out ready for cutting as in figure 37; in this way you will achieve a continuous grain effect.

For this box any corner joint could be used, depending on the skill of the maker. I chose the lapped butt joint (figure 38) which is a fairly strong and neat joint, while at the same time being easy to make. For those less experienced, the straightforward butt joint (figure 39) could be used; this needs to be glued and nailed. If cramps are not available, both these joints need to be glued and nailed using panel pins. If cramps are available it is sufficient for a box of this size to glue only the lapped butt joint. When panel pins are used for this purpose, they are put in at an angle. This is called skew nailing or dovetail nailing, as the angle of the nails makes it more difficult for the work to be pulled apart and gives a stronger joint (figure 40). For the more advanced woodworker one of the dovetail joints would make a satisfying alternative.

The sides are not sawn to size, and if the butt joint is to be used instead of the lapped butt joint, the two end pieces will

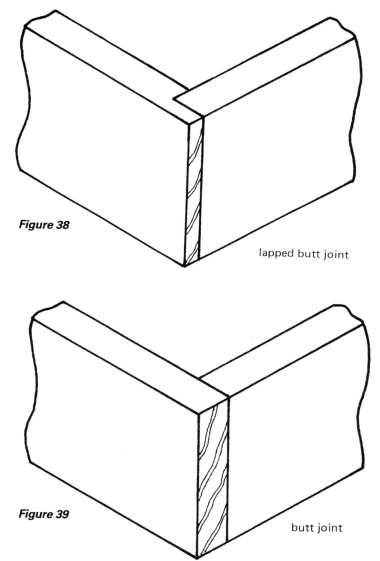

Figure 38

lapped butt joint

Figure 39

butt joint

need to be sawn to 3¼ in (81 mm) long instead of 4 in (100 mm). For either of these joints, it is important that each end of the end pieces of the box is sawn square, so that a good fit is obtained when the box is assembled. If the lapped butt joint is used, mark it out and cut it out on the two side pieces of the box.

Base

Test the box for fit and when you are satisfied prepare the base from a piece of matching wood 7 × 3¼ × ⅝ in (175 × 81 × 15 mm) so that it fits neatly into the base of the box as shown in figure 41. Mark 1½ in (37.5 mm) along each side of the base and drill a hole ⅛ in (3 mm) in diameter and ¾ in (18 mm) deep to take a 1 in (25 mm) steel rod, ⅛ in (3 mm) in diameter,

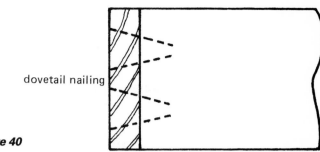

dovetail nailing

Figure 40

which will allow the base to pivot in the box. Mark out the sides of the box and drill with the ⅛ in (3 mm) drill ¼ in (6 mm) deep to receive the steel rod. Assemble the box with the base in and check that the base pivots freely.

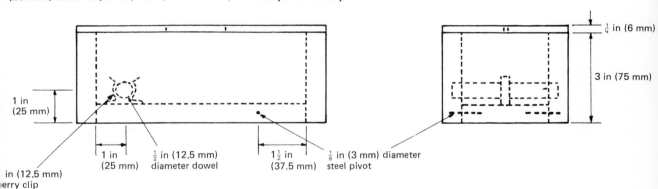

1 in (25 mm)

1 in (25 mm)

½ in (12.5 mm) diameter dowel

1½ in (37.5 mm)

⅛ in (3 mm) diameter steel pivot

in (12.5 mm) erry clip

¼ in (6 mm)

3 in (75 mm)

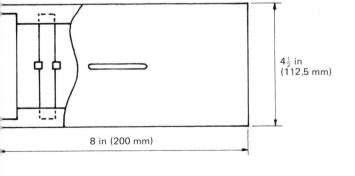

4½ in (112.5 mm)

8 in (200 mm)

Figure 41

Locking mechanism

For the locking mechanism you will need to drill a ½ in (12.5 mm) diameter hole on the inside of each side of the box to a depth of ¼ in (6 mm) to the dimensions shown in figure 41. Cut a piece of ½ in (12.5 mm) dowel to 3¾ in (93 mm) long and fit it into the holes in the sides. Position a ½ in (12.5 mm) Terry clip centrally onto the dowel and mark its position on the base. Screw it to the base using a ½ in (12.5 mm) no. 4 round-head brass screw. Check that the locking mechanism operates smoothly. Finally, assemble the box with the base in position, using glue and panel pins if necessary.

Top

For the top you will need a piece of plywood 8 × 4½ × ¼ in (200 × 112.5 × 6 mm). Mark out a slot for the coins in the centre of the box measuring 1½ × ⅛ in (37.5 × 3 mm). Drill this out using a ⅛ in (3 mm) diameter drill and clean it up using a small file and glasspaper. Now glue the top onto the box. If you don't have cramps you will also need to use panel pins although it is much better if this can be avoided, as they will need to be filled afterwards and will tend to spoil the finished look of the box. Plane down the sides of the top to a flush fit with the box.

Finishing

Clean up the box using glasspaper in preparation for the finish. A varnish finish will look attractive and can be decorated with transfers or a painted design.

The box is opened by turning it upside down and pressing firmly with the thumbs on the pivoted end.

11. Treasure Chest

Materials

Carcase

Sides: 2 off 4¾ × 3¼ × ⁵⁄₁₆ in (118 × 81 × 7.5 mm) softwood

Top and bottom: 2 off 2¾ × 3 × ⁵⁄₁₆ in (68 × 75 × 7.5 mm) softwood

Back: 1 off 4¾ × 2¾ × ¼ in (118 × 68 × 6 mm) softwood

Base: 1 off 3⅝ × 3⅜ × ⁵⁄₁₆ in (90 × 84 × 7.5 mm) softwood

Top: 1 off 3⅞ × 3½ × ⁵⁄₁₆ in (96 × 87.5 × 7.5 mm) softwood

Drawer

Front and back: 2 off 2¾ × 1¼ × ½ in (68 × 31 × 12.5 mm) softwood

Sides: 2 off 2¼ × 1¼ × ¼ in (56 × 31 × 6 mm) softwood

Base: 1 off 2½ × 2¼ × ¼ in (62.5 × 56 × 6 mm) softwood

Runners: 2 off 2½ × ¼ × ⅛ in (62.5 × 6 × 3 mm) softwood

Stops: 2 off ½ × ¼ × ⅛ in (12.5 × 6 × 3 mm) softwood

Catch: 1 off 1¾ × ⅜ × ¹⁄₁₆ in (43 × 9 × 1.5 mm) aluminium

False drawer front: 1 off 2¹³⁄₁₆ × 2¾ × ½ in (69.5 × 68 × 12.5 mm) softwood

Drawer handles: 3 off ⅞ × ¼ × ³⁄₁₆ in (21 × 6 × 4.5 mm) softwood

3 off ½ in (12.5 mm) no. 4 round-head brass screws

2 off ½ in (12.5 mm) panel pins

1 elastic band

adhesive

varnish

Figure 42

Tools

marking knife
try square
marking gauge
tenon saw
hand drill
half-round smooth file
hammer
G cramp
rebate plane
jack plane
bradawl
screwdriver
cork rubber
glasspaper

This attractive little box with its hidden secrets will amaze and amuse both young and old alike. The two lower drawers in the box are false. Only the top drawer opens, and when an object such as a coin is placed in the drawer it can be made mysteriously to disappear by shutting and opening the drawer. Once the coin has disappeared it cannot be made to

reappear, because the drawer cannot be removed until you have mastered the second secret of the treasure chest.

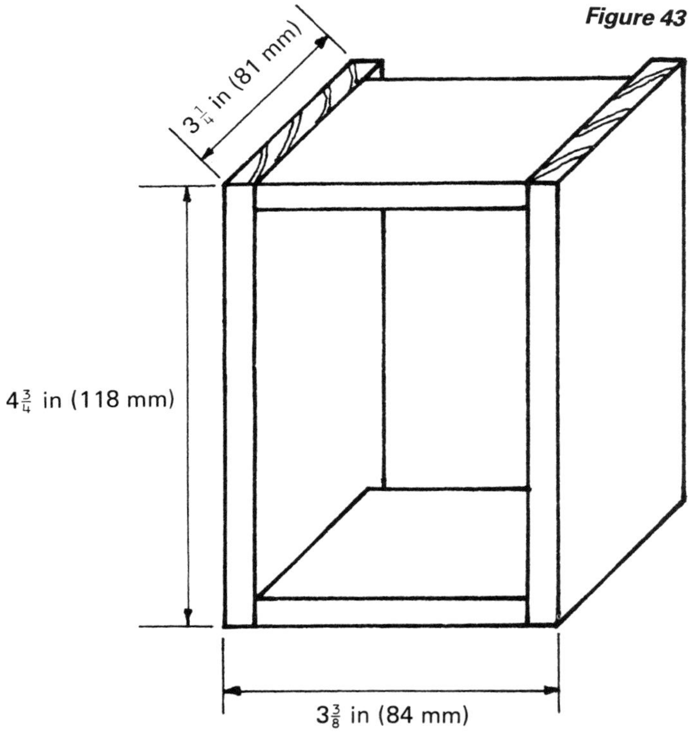

Carcase

For the sides of the carcase you will need two pieces of softwood 4¾ × 3¼ × ⁵⁄₁₆ in (118 × 81 × 7.5 mm); if you prefer, the whole box could be made from a suitable hardwood if one is available. The top and bottom of the carcase are made from two pieces of softwood 2¾ × 3 × ⁵⁄₁₆ in (68 × 75 × 7.5 mm).

Carefully clean up the sides and accurately square off the ends. Use a try square and marking knife to mark out, then saw to size using a tenon saw. As this is a small item, it is necessary to be very accurate with your measuring, as inaccuracies are clearly seen with this type of work. Glue the sides and the top and bottom together as shown in figure 43. It is possible to do this carefully without using nails, if you have G cramps available: simply glue and cramp up the carcase.

Before the glue is applied to the butt joints, it is a good idea to cramp up the work dry and check that the carcase goes together squarely. When you are satisfied with your work, glue and cramp it together. If G cramps are not available then the butt joints will have to be glued and pinned using ¾ in (18 mm) panel pins.

The back of the carcase is cut from a piece of softwood to measure 4¾ × 2¾ × ¼ in (118 × 68 × 6 mm). Cut it so that it fits tightly into the back of the box after the carcase has been glued. When a good fit has been obtained, glue the back in position as shown in figure 44.

Base

The base is made from a piece of softwood 3⅝ × 3⅜ × ⁵⁄₁₆ in (90 × 84 × 7.5 mm). Cut a ⅛ in (3 mm) chamfer on the front and both sides using a plane, or, if this is not available, radius the edge with a half-round smooth file (figure 45). Glue the base accurately to the bottom of the box. The back of the base must lie flush

Figure 43

3¼ in (81 mm)

4¾ in (118 mm)

3⅜ in (84 mm)

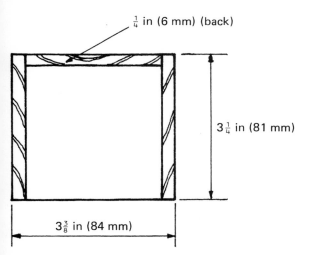

$\frac{1}{4}$ in (6 mm) (back)

$3\frac{1}{4}$ in (81 mm)

$3\frac{3}{8}$ in (84 mm)

Figure 44

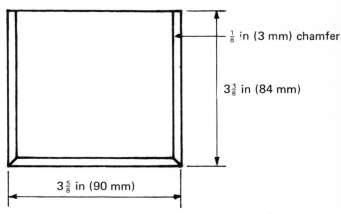

$\frac{1}{8}$ in (3 mm) chamfer

$3\frac{3}{8}$ in (84 mm)

$3\frac{5}{8}$ in (90 mm)

Figure 45

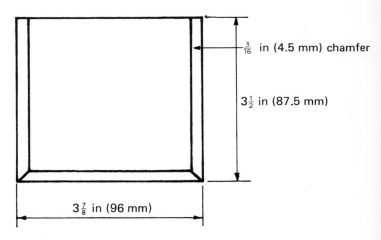

$\frac{3}{16}$ in (4.5 mm) chamfer

$3\frac{1}{2}$ in (87.5 mm)

$3\frac{7}{8}$ in (96 mm)

Figure 46

with the back of the carcase. Then either cramp or pin in position. If you cramp the work in position, check as you tighten up the cramp that the base does not move.

Cabinet top

The cabinet top is made from a piece of softwood 3⅞ × 3½ × ⁵⁄₁₆ in (96 × 87.5 × 7.5 mm). Finish it to the sides and back with a ³⁄₁₆ in (4.5 mm) chamfer (figure 46). Glue the cabinet top in position with the cabinet top flush with the back of the cabinet.

Drawer

For the front and back drawer you will need two pieces of softwood 2¾ × 1¼ × ½ in (68 × 31 × 12.5 mm). For the sides you will need two pieces of softwood (2¼ × 1¼ × ¼ in (56 × 31 × 6 mm). For the base you will need a piece of softwood 2½ × 2¼ × ¼ in (62.5 × 56 × 6 mm).

Figure 47 shows the plan view of the drawer. Cut rebates on both ends of the front and back ¼ × ¼ in (6 × 6 mm) to receive the sides as shown. When this is done, cut the bottom rebates in all four drawer sides. These will be ¼ × ¼ in (6 × 6 mm) on the front and back of the drawer and ¼ × ⅛ in (6 × 3 mm) on the two sides of the drawer. Do this with a rebate plane.

43

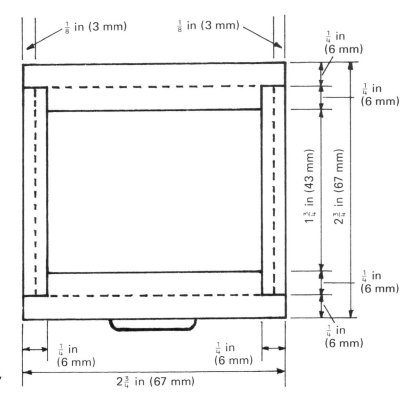

$\frac{1}{8}$ in (3 mm) $\frac{1}{8}$ in (3 mm)

$\frac{1}{4}$ in (6 mm)

$\frac{1}{4}$ in (6 mm)

$1\frac{3}{4}$ in (43 mm)

$2\frac{3}{4}$ in (67 mm)

$\frac{1}{4}$ in (6 mm)

$\frac{1}{4}$ in (6 mm)

$\frac{1}{4}$ in (6 mm) $\frac{1}{4}$ in (6 mm)

Figure 47 $2\frac{3}{4}$ in (67 mm)

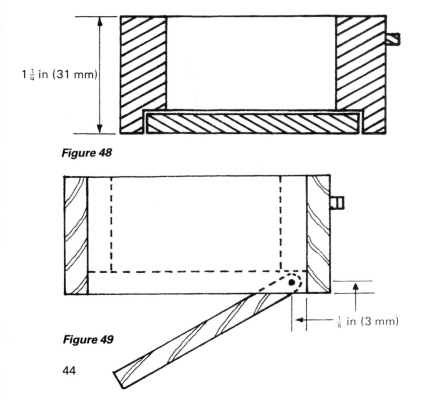

$1\frac{1}{4}$ in (31 mm)

Figure 48

Figure 49 $\frac{1}{8}$ in (3 mm)

If you do not have one, set a marking gauge to the dimensions given and mark out the rebates using the marking gauge. Then cut them out with a tenon saw and neaten them with glasspaper.

The drawer is now ready to glue up. Glue without pins if you have G cramps. Cramp without glue first, to check that the drawer is square and accurate and then glue when it is satisfactory. Now adjust the bottom of the drawer so that it fits loosely in the bottom rebates of the drawer as in figure 48. Radius the front end of the bottom of the drawer. Place the base in the rebate and mark out and drill the pivot hole through the sides for the base of the drawer (figure 49); then tap in a ½ in (12.5 mm) panel pin on each side so

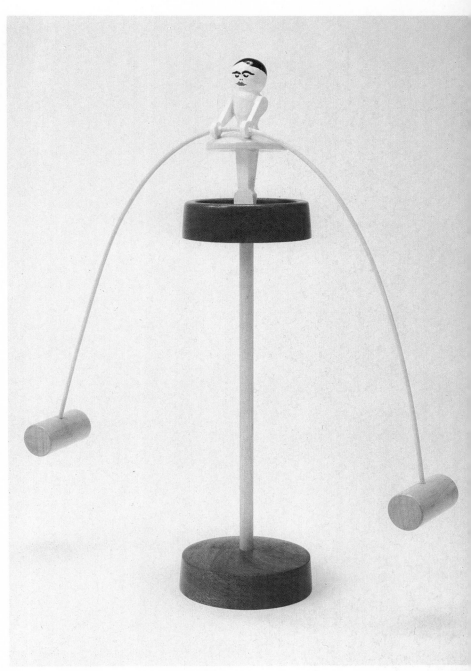

Dancing Ballerina

Somersaulting Man

Exploding Destroyer

Secret Money Box

that the bottom of the drawer pivots freely. Do not fully drive the pins in until you are sure that the bottom of the drawer will fall down freely. It may be necessary to remove the drawer bottom once or twice and ease it with glasspaper until this is achieved. When you are satisfied, drive in the panel pins so that they finish flush with the sides.

Drawer catch

For the drawer catch you will need a piece of aluminium 1¾ × ⅜ × ¹⁄₁₆ in (43 × 9 × 1.5 mm). Mark out as in figure 50 and drill two holes ⅛ in (3 mm) in diameter as shown. Bend the catch slightly and assemble it on the back of the drawer (figure 51). Put a suitable elastic band through the top hole of the catch and secure it to the screw. The screws used are ½ in (12.5 mm) no. 4 round-head brass screws. Adjust the pivoting screw so that the catch can move freely and remain in the position shown when it is under the tension of the elastic band.

Drawer runners

The drawer runners are made from two pieces of softwood 2½ × ¼ × ⅛ in (62.5 × 6 × 3 mm). Glue these to the sides of the box parallel to the top, so that the drawer will run smoothly on them (figure 52). The easiest way to do this is to place the drawer in position and then glue the runners in, so that the drawer runs freely. It will be necessary to glue in a little block of softwood each side at the back of the runner to act as a drawer stop, so that when the drawer is in the closed position the drawer front finishes flush with the front of the cabinet.

False drawer fronts

The false drawer front is made from a piece of softwood 2¹³⁄₁₆ × 2¾ × ½ in (69.5 × 68 × 12.5 mm). Put a saw cut across the front 1⅜ in (34 mm) down to a depth of ⅛ in (3 mm) (figure 53). Use a tenon saw for this. This gives the effect of two drawers. The inside top edge of the drawer front is

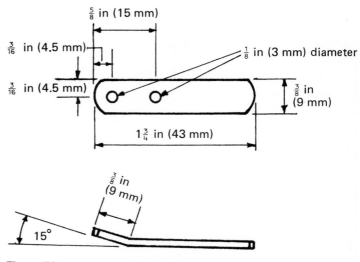

Figure 50

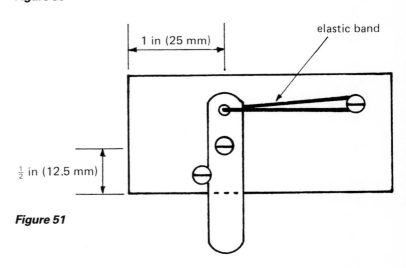

Figure 51

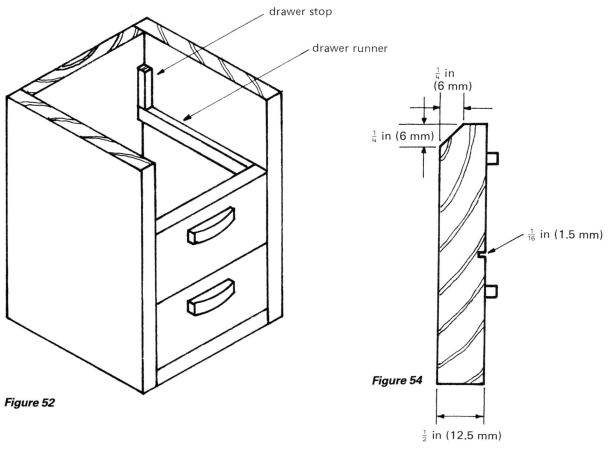

drawer stop

drawer runner

Figure 52

$\frac{1}{4}$ in (6 mm)

$\frac{1}{4}$ in (6 mm)

$\frac{1}{16}$ in (1.5 mm)

Figure 54

$\frac{1}{2}$ in (12.5 mm)

Figure 53

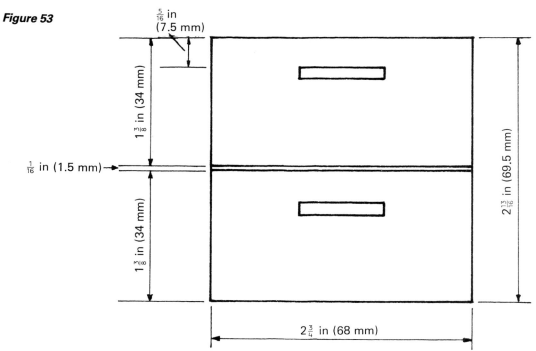

$\frac{5}{16}$ in (7.5 mm)

$1\frac{3}{8}$ in (34 mm)

$\frac{1}{16}$ in (1.5 mm)

$1\frac{3}{8}$ in (34 mm)

$2\frac{13}{16}$ in (69.5 mm)

$2\frac{3}{4}$ in (68 mm)

chamfered ¼ × ¼ in (6 × 6 mm) (figure 54); this is to allow the bottom of the drawer to drop down when the drawer is in the closed position. Glue the false drawer front in position as shown in figure 52. Cut and glue three small handles to the drawer fronts. Put the drawer catch in the neutral position and place the top drawer in the chest.

Finishing

The treasure chest can now be cleaned up with glasspaper and prepared for the finish. A basic varnish will enhance the appearance of the wood and will be a suitable background for a decorative finish such as a painted design or transfer.

Solution

As the top drawer is pulled out, the base of the drawer swings up into the closed position. When an object is put into it and the drawer is closed, the bottom of the drawer falls down so that the object 'disappears' into the bottom of the chest. As the catch will not allow the drawer to be pulled out, the object cannot be retrieved without the catch being put into the neutral position. This is done by inserting a thin-bladed knife beneath the base of the top drawer in the closed position and swinging the catch so that the drawer can be pulled out.

12. Submarine

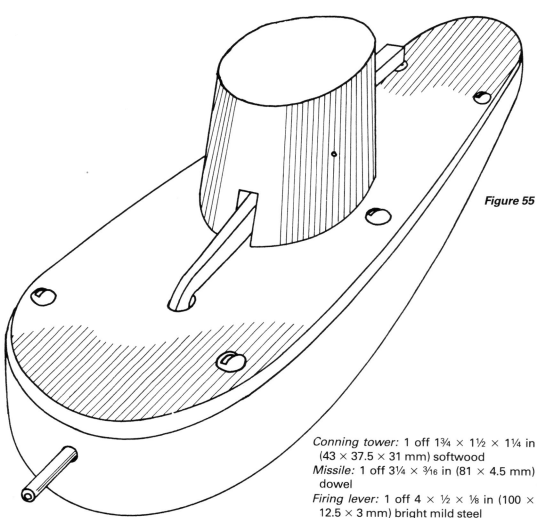

Figure 55

Materials

Hull: 1 off 9 × 2½ × 1 in (225 mm × 62.5 × 25 mm) softwood

Deck: 1 off 9 × 2½ × ³⁄₁₆ in (225 × 62.5 × 4.5 mm) birch ply

Plunger: 1 off 1⅛ × ½ × ½ in (28 × 12.5 × 12.5 mm) hardwood

Conning tower: 1 off 1¾ × 1½ × 1¼ in (43 × 37.5 × 31 mm) softwood

Missile: 1 off 3¼ × ³⁄₁₆ in (81 × 4.5 mm) dowel

Firing lever: 1 off 4 × ½ × ⅛ in (100 × 12.5 × 3 mm) bright mild steel

Pivot rod: 1 off 1½ in (37.5 mm) wire nail

2 off ¾ in (18 mm) wire nails

2 off ⅝ in (15 mm) no. 4 countersunk steel screws

6 off ½ in (12.5 mm) no. 4 round-head brass screws

1 off 2¼ × ¼ in (56 × 6 mm) elastic band

enamel paint

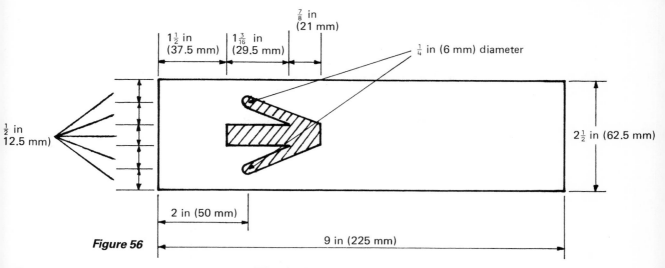

$\frac{7}{8}$ in
(21 mm)

$1\frac{1}{2}$ in
(37.5 mm)

$1\frac{3}{16}$ in
(29.5 mm)

$\frac{1}{4}$ in (6 mm) diameter

$\frac{1}{2}$ in
12.5 mm)

$2\frac{1}{2}$ in (62.5 mm)

2 in (50 mm)

9 in (225 mm)

Figure 56

Tools

try square	hacksaw
tenon saw	chisel
coping saw	mallet
hand drill	bradawl
$\frac{3}{32}$ in (2.25 mm) drill	screwdriver
$\frac{1}{4}$ in (6 mm) drill	cork rubber
half-round file	glasspaper

This little model is very exciting to make and appeals to young and old alike. The simple firing mechanism which will launch a missile adds to the realism of the model and to the enjoyment of using it. The basic design shown here lends itself to further modifications and development, and I have found that with this model the temptation to make more models, each with a slight modification and improvement, is strong. You must remember, when using the model, never to point it at anyone, as the firing mechanism is quite effective and projects the missile with a fair amount of force, which could cause an accident if you are not careful.

The hull

For the hull you will need a piece of softwood 9 × 2½ × 1 in (225 × 62.5 × 25 mm) which is marked out as in figure 56. Cut out the shaded area to a depth of ½ in (12.5 mm). Start this operation by drilling the two ¼ in (6 mm) diameter holes, and then carefully and accurately cut out the wood with a chisel as shown in the drawing. This area will house the firing mechanism. It is essential that the bottom of the recess in particular is as flat and as smooth as possible to give a good firing action.

When this has been completed, drill a ¼ in (6 mm) hole (figures 57, 58) for the missile. Now hammer two ¾ in (18 mm) wire nails into the recess as shown in figures 57 and 58 so that the head of the nail is just

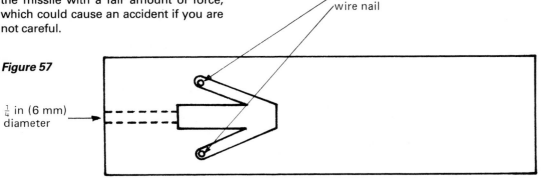

$\frac{3}{4}$ in (18 mm)
wire nail

Figure 57

$\frac{1}{4}$ in (6 mm)
diameter

49

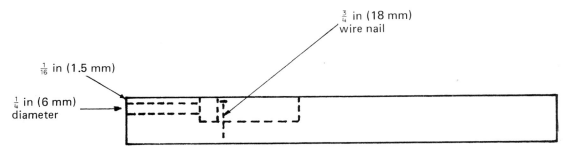

$\frac{3}{4}$ in (18 mm)
wire nail

$\frac{1}{16}$ in (1.5 mm)

$\frac{1}{4}$ in (6 mm) diameter

Figure 58

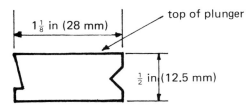

$1\frac{1}{8}$ in (28 mm)

top of plunger

$\frac{1}{2}$ in (12.5 mm)

Figure 59

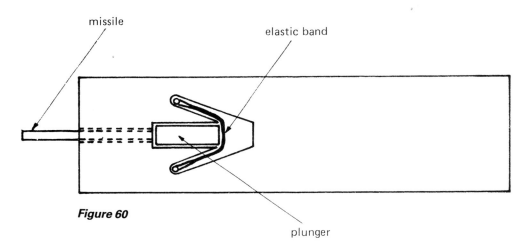

missile

elastic band

plunger

Figure 60

below the surface. These nails will hold the elastic band for the firing mechanism. Take care when you do this that the nails are hammered in vertically. The outside of the hull is not shaped at this stage.

The plunger

The plunger is best made from a piece of hardwood $1\frac{1}{8} \times \frac{1}{2} \times \frac{1}{2}$ in (28 × 12.5 × 12.5 mm). Cut it to size and shape it by filing (figure 59). Smooth the plunger with

glasspaper so that it runs freely in the recess made for it in the hull (figure 60). Take a $2\frac{1}{4} \times \frac{1}{4}$ in (56 × 6 mm) elastic band and loop it over the nails with the V cut of the plunger in position against the elastic band (figure 60). Cut the missile from a piece of dowel $3\frac{1}{4} \times \frac{3}{16}$ in (78 × 4.5 mm).

The strength of the firing mechanism is controlled by the type of elastic band used and you may find it necessary to experiment with different elastic bands until you are satisfied with its performance.

Figure 61

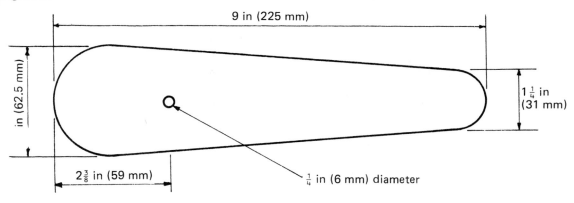

9 in (225 mm)

in (62.5 mm)

$1\frac{1}{4}$ in (31 mm)

$2\frac{3}{8}$ in (59 mm)

$\frac{1}{4}$ in (6 mm) diameter

Figure 62

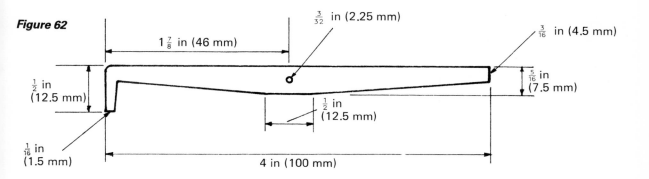

$\frac{3}{32}$ in (2.25 mm)

$\frac{3}{16}$ in (4.5 mm)

$1\frac{7}{8}$ in (46 mm)

$\frac{5}{16}$ in (7.5 mm)

$\frac{1}{2}$ in (12.5 mm)

$\frac{1}{2}$ in (12.5 mm)

$\frac{1}{16}$ in (1.5 mm)

4 in (100 mm)

The deck

The deck is made from a piece of plywood 9 × 2½ × 3/16 in (225 × 62.5 × 4.5 mm). Mark it out and drill with a ¼ in (6 mm) drill as shown in figure 61. Cut it to the deck shape using a coping saw and finish it off with a file and glasspaper.

Firing lever

The firing lever is made from a piece of mild steel 4 × ½ × ⅛ in (100 × 12.5 × 3 mm). Cut with a hacksaw and file to the shape shown in figure 62. Drill a hole 3/32 in (2.25 mm) to take a 1½ in (37.5 mm) wire nail, on which the bar will pivot when it is fitted to the conning tower. Remove the

head from the wire nail with a hacksaw before using it as the pivot for the lever.

Conning tower

Cut the conning tower from a piece of wood 1¾ × 1½ × 1¼ in (43 × 37.5 × 31 mm). Before shaping the conning tower you must cut a slot using a tenon saw to take the firing lever, so that the lever can pivot up and down freely (figure 63). Next drill the hole for the pivot bar on which the firing lever pivots. Now shape the wood to an oval to represent the conning tower, using a smooth file and glasspaper. Fit the firing lever in position in the conning tower and file the pivot rod flush at each side.

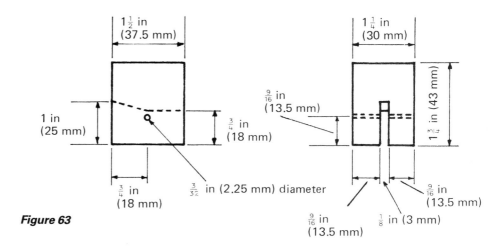

$1\frac{1}{2}$ in
(37.5 mm)

1 in
(25 mm)

$\frac{3}{4}$ in
(18 mm)

$\frac{3}{4}$ in
(18 mm)

$\frac{3}{32}$ in (2.25 mm) diameter

Figure 63

$1\frac{1}{4}$ in
(30 mm)

$\frac{9}{16}$ in
(13.5 mm)

$1\frac{3}{4}$ in (43 mm)

$\frac{9}{16}$ in
(13.5 mm)

$\frac{9}{16}$ in
(13.5 mm)

$\frac{1}{8}$ in (3 mm)

Figure 64

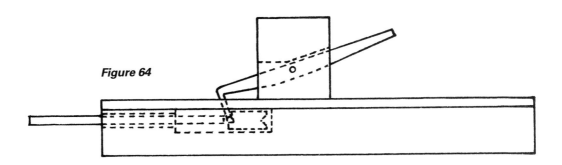

Place the deck and conning tower in position on the hull and hold in place so that the firing mechanism can be tested by inserting the missile and pushing it into the loaded position (figure 64). When you have found the correct position for the conning tower and deck, mark with a pencil the position of the conning tower on the deck, then screw the conning tower in position with two ⅝ in (15 mm) no. 4 countersunk steel screws, from under the deck up into the conning tower.

Reposition the deck on the hull, mark the deck shape onto the hull and cut the hull to shape with a coping saw. Screw the deck to the hull using six ½ in (12.5 mm) no. 4 round-head brass screws.

Finishing

Once again, check that the firing mechanism works before finally shaping the hull by filing and glasspapering to suit the deck shape. Using glasspaper, clean up the submarine to a smooth finish in readiness for painting. The submarine looks particularly realistic if finished in a grey gloss with suitable transfers added.

13. Exploding Destroyer

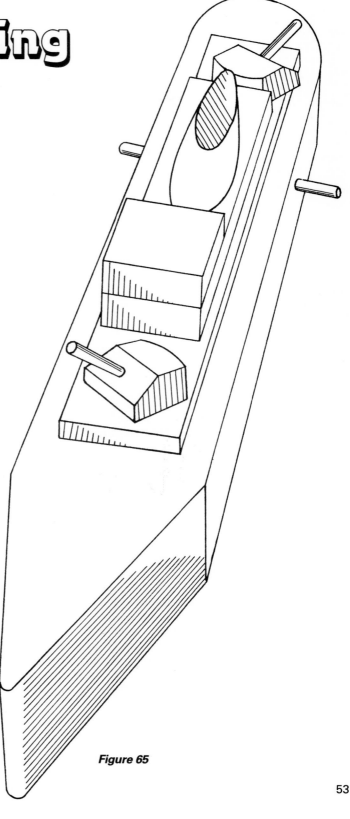

Materials

Hull: 1 off 12 × 2⅜ × 1 in (300 × 59 × 25 mm) softwood

Firing pin: 2 off 1¾ × ¼ in (43 × 6 mm) dowel

Firing lever: 1 off 2¾ × ¼ × ⅛ in (68 × 6 × 3 mm) bright mild steel

Pivoting rod: 1 off 2⅜ × 1/16 in (59 × 1.5 mm) steel rod

Packing pieces: 2 off ⅛ × ⅜ in (3 × 9 mm) polythene tube

1 off ⅝ in (15 mm) no. 4 round-head brass screw

1 off ¾ in (18 mm) panel pin

1 off 2¼ × ¼ in (56 × 6 mm) elastic band

Superstructure

Base: 1 off 6 × 1¼ × 5/16 in (150 × 31 × 7.5 mm) softwood

2 off ½ × 3/16 in (12.5 × 4.5 mm) dowel

Cabin and bridge: 1 off 4¾ × 1¼ × ½ in (118 × 31 × 12.5 mm) softwood

Gun turrets: 2 off 1 × 1 × ½ in (25 × 25 × 12.5 mm) softwood

Guns: 2 off 1 × 3/16 in (25 × 4.5 mm) dowel

Funnel: 1 off 1¼ × 1¼ × ¾ in (31 × 31 × 18 mm) softwood

enamel paint

Tools

try square	centre punch
tenon saw	junior hacksaw
coping saw	chisel
hand drill	mallet
1/16 in (1.5 mm) drill	hammer
⅛ in (3 mm) drill	bradawl
3/16 in (4.5 mm) drill	screwdriver
¼ in (6 mm) drill	cork rubber
5/16 in (7.5 mm) drill	glasspaper
half-round file	

Figure 65

53

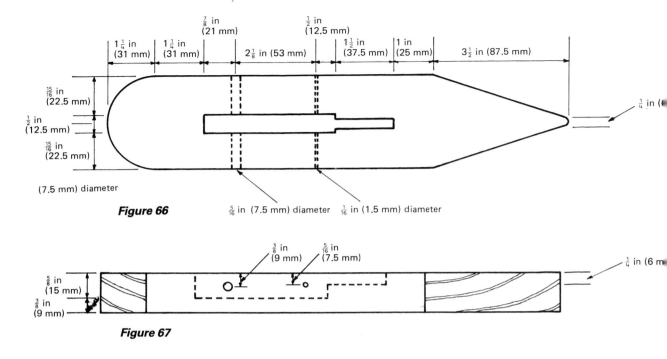

$\frac{7}{8}$ in (21 mm)

$\frac{1}{2}$ in (12.5 mm)

$1\frac{1}{4}$ in (31 mm) $1\frac{1}{4}$ in (31 mm) $2\frac{1}{8}$ in (53 mm) $1\frac{1}{2}$ in (37.5 mm) 1 in (25 mm) $3\frac{1}{2}$ in (87.5 mm)

$\frac{15}{16}$ in (22.5 mm)

$\frac{1}{2}$ in (12.5 mm)

$\frac{15}{16}$ in (22.5 mm)

$\frac{1}{4}$ in (

(7.5 mm) diameter

Figure 66

$\frac{5}{16}$ in (7.5 mm) diameter $\frac{1}{16}$ in (1.5 mm) diameter

$\frac{3}{8}$ in (9 mm) $\frac{5}{16}$ in (7.5 mm)

$\frac{1}{4}$ in (6 m

$\frac{9}{16}$ in (15 mm)

$\frac{3}{8}$ in (9 mm)

Figure 67

When you have made the missile-firing submarine, you will want to add to your fleet with this model of an exploding destroyer. When the firing pins situated on either side of the hull are hit, the superstructure of the destroyer will be flung into the air as though the whole boat has exploded. With practice and a good aim, the missile from the submarine can explode the destroyer.

The destroyer is constructed so that the gun turrets swivel on their mountings, and even without employing the firing mechanism, this delightful model encourages imaginative play. The mechanism could also be adapted to a number of other models where a realistic exploding effect would add to the pleasure of the toy. This model is made from softwood as the explosive effect is heightened when a lighter wood is used.

The hull

The hull is made from a piece of softwood 12 × 2⅜ × 1 in (300 × 59 × 25 mm) and is marked out as shown in figures 66 and 67. You will need a try square to ensure that the marking out is accurate. Next, cut out the slot for the mechanism with a chisel to a depth of ⅝ in (15 mm) and ½ in (12.5 mm) wide for the large slot; the smaller part of the slot is cut to a depth of ¼ in (6 mm) and ¼ in (6 mm) wide.

Turn the hull on its side and mark out the centre for the 5⁄16 in (7.5 mm) diameter hole and the 1⁄16 in (1.5 mm) diameter hole in preparation for drilling. Drill the 5⁄16 in (7.5 mm) diameter hole right through the width of the wood. This will house the firing pins. The 1⁄16 in (1.5 mm) diameter hole is drilled through the hull and this will house the pivoting rod for the firing lever. You must drill these holes accurately so that the firing mechanism will operate smoothly in use.

Next, saw the bow to shape with a tenon saw and lightly round the pointed end of the bow with a half-round smooth file. Cut the stern to shape with a coping saw and acquire the final shape with a half-round smooth file.

Firing pins

For the firing pins take two pieces of ¼ in (6 mm) diameter dowel and cut to 1¾ in (43 mm) long. These will be placed one on each side in the 5⁄16 in (7.5 mm) diameter holes drilled in the hull, and they should move freely. It may be necessary to glasspaper them lightly to give a smooth action.

Firing lever

The firing lever is made from a piece of bright mild steel 2¾ × ¼ × ⅛ in (68 × 6 × 3 mm) and is marked out as in figure 68. Mark out the centres to the dimensions given, centre punch and drill with an ⅛ in (3 mm) diameter drill. Round one end with a half-round smooth file, cut the other end to shape with a junior hacksaw and finish

with the file. Cut the pivoting rod from a piece of 1⁄16 in (1.5 mm) diameter rod to a length of 2⅜ in (59 mm). This will give a loose fit in the firing lever which is necessary for the efficient working of the mechanism: when the firing pins touch the lever, a sideways movement of the lever is necessary to release it so that it will spring up and project the super-structure upwards and away from the hull.

Before assembling the firing lever in the slot of the hull, cut two packing pieces ⅛ in (3 mm) long from a ⅜ in (9 mm) diameter piece of polythene tube. These packing pieces should be approximately ⅛ in (3 mm) wide and will be placed one each side of the firing lever in the slot, so that the firing lever lies in the centre along the slot (figure 69).

Figure 68

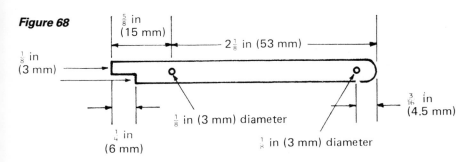

⅝ in (15 mm)

2⅛ in (53 mm)

⅛ in (3 mm)

3⁄16 in (4.5 mm)

⅛ in (3 mm) diameter

¼ in (6 mm)

¼ in (3 mm) diameter

Figure 69

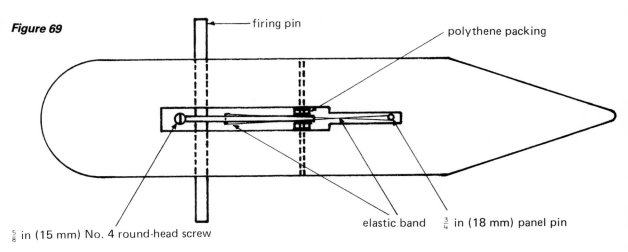

firing pin

polythene packing

elastic band

¾ in (18 mm) panel pin

⅝ in (15 mm) No. 4 round-head screw

55

Assemble the firing lever and packing pieces in the slot and push the pivot rod right in. A ⅝ in (15 mm) no. 4 round-head brass screw is screwed into position in the slot so that the firing lever just catches under the head of the screw. Position a ¾ in (18 mm) panel pin in the ¼ × ¼ in (6 × 6mm) slot as in figure 69. Then thread a 2¼ × ¼ in (56 × 6 mm) elastic band through the hole in the lever and hook it over the panel pin, bending over the head of the panel pin slightly to secure the elastic band.

When the lever is pushed down in position under the head of the screw, it should be in a position of tension. Then, when the firing pins are pushed in from either side, the lever will be released so that it springs back towards the panel pin. Check this movement so that the lightest touch on the firing pins will release the firing lever. For fine adjustment of the firing lever it may be necessary lightly to file the end to make it more sensitive when touched by the firing pins.

Superstructure

The base of the superstructure is cut from a piece of softwood 6 × 1¼ × ⁵⁄₁₆ in (150 × 31 × 7.5 mm). Drill ³⁄₁₆ in (4.5 mm) diameter holes half way through, according to the dimensions given in figure 70. Cut two pieces of ³⁄₁₆ in (4.5 mm) diameter dowel ½ in (12.5 mm) long and glue into the holes on which the gun turrets will rotate. Then cut the cabin 3½ × 1 in (87 × 25 mm) and the bridge 1¼ × 1 in (31× 25 mm) from a piece of softwood 4¾ × 1 × ½ in (118 × 25 × 12.5 mm) (figure 71).

Cut each gun turret from a piece of softwood 1 × 1 × ½ in (25 × 25 × 12.5 mm), shape and drill them (figure 72). Make the guns from a 1 in (25 mm) piece of ³⁄₁₆ in (4.5 mm) diameter dowel and glue them into position in the turrets. Make the funnel from a piece of softwood 1¼ × 1¼ × ¾ in (31 × 31 × 18 mm). Suitably shape the funnel using a half-round smooth file and glasspaper to the dimensions given in figure 73.

Finishing

You are now ready to clean up both the hull and superstructure. Use glasspaper, smoothing the work to a good finish in preparation for painting. Like the submarine, the destroyer will look particularly effective if finished with a base of grey gloss enamel paint. Different parts of the superstructure can be highlighted with contrasting colours and completed with transfers.

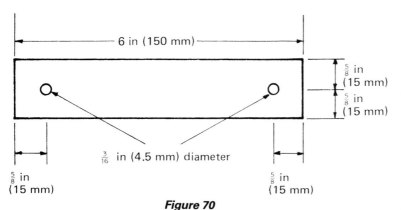

Figure 70

Figure 71

Figure 72

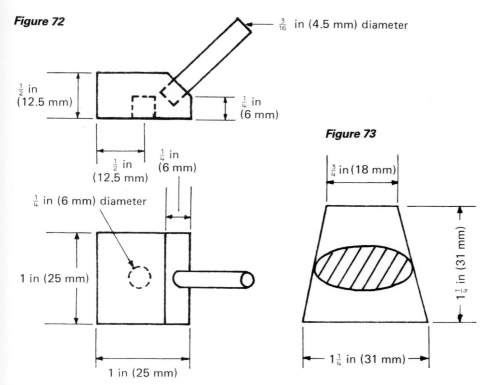

$\frac{3}{16}$ in (4.5 mm) diameter

$\frac{1}{2}$ in
(12.5 mm)

$\frac{1}{4}$ in
(6 mm)

$\frac{1}{2}$ in
(12.5 mm)

$\frac{1}{4}$ in
(6 mm)

$\frac{1}{4}$ in (6 mm) diameter

1 in (25 mm)

1 in (25 mm)

Figure 73

$\frac{3}{4}$ in (18 mm)

$1\frac{1}{4}$ in (31 mm)

$1\frac{1}{4}$ in (31 mm)

14. Shaking Sidney

Materials

Track: 1 off 28³⁄₁₆ × 3¾ × ½ in (704.5 × 93 × 12.5 mm) plywood
Pegs: 63 off 1 × ¼ in (25 ×6 mm) dowel
Stand: 2 off 5½ × 3 × ½ in (137.5 × 75 × 12.5 mm) plywood
1 off 2¾ × 2 × ½ in (68 × 50 × 12.5 mm) plywood
Shaking Sidney: 1 off 4½ × 3 in (112.5 × 75 mm) hardboard or ¼ in (6 mm) plywood
1 in (25 mm) panel pins
adhesive
varnish
enamel paint

Tools

tenon saw
fret saw or coping saw
hand drill
¼ in (6 mm) drill
hammer
nail punch
jack plane
cork rubber
glasspaper

With his bright colours and movement Shaking Sidney will both amuse and fascinate you. The rhythmic clicking caused by Sidney shaking himself from peg to peg adds to the pleasure of this model. To start Sidney shaking, simply place him at the top of the track to set him in action. This is an easily made toy, but it does need a fair degree of accuracy for Sidney to shake comfortably down the pegs. The interest of the toy is enhanced if a partner is made for Shaking Sidney, so that they can chase each other down the track.

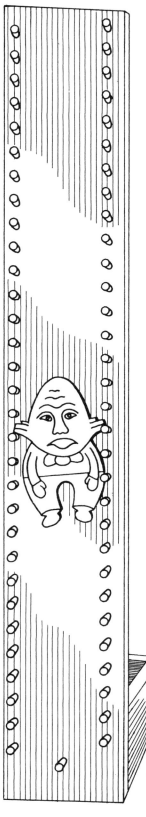

Figure 74

Track

The track is made from a piece of ½ in (12.5 mm) plywood, 28 × 3¾ in (700 × 93 mm). Square up the wood and mark out as in figure 75. The marking out has to be accurate and the easy way to do this is to use a marking gauge set to ½ in (12.5 mm) and gauge down the full length on each side of the back of the track. Then, take a pair of dividers, set them to ⅞ in (21 mm), and step off the measurement all the way down. This should give you 31 centres down each side. Drill these holes as accurately as possible with a ¼ in (6 mm) drill.

Cut 62 1 in (25 mm) pieces of ¼ in (6 mm) diameter dowel. Clean up the track with glasspaper, lightly round one end of each dowel with glasspaper, and then glue the dowels in position. At the foot of the track, drill a ¼ in (6 mm) hole in the centre, 1¼ in (31 mm) up from the base, as shown in figure 75. Cut another 1 in (25 mm) piece of ¼ in (6 mm) diameter dowel and glue it into this position to act as a stop for Shaking Sidney.

Stand

For the stand you will need two pieces of ¼ in (12.5 mm) plywood 5½ x 3 in (137.5 x 75 mm). Mark these out and cut to the shape shown in figure 76. You will also need another piece of plywood 2¾ x 2 in (68 x 50 mm) for the back of the stand. Clean these up with glasspaper and glue and pin them together using 1 in (25 mm) panel pins as shown in figure 76. Glue and pin the stand and track together.

Shaking Sidney

Shaking Sidney is made from a piece of hardboard or ¼ in (6 mm) plywod, measuring 4½ x 3 in (112.5 x 75 mm). Mark this out into ½ in (12.5 mm) squares and mark out Sidney as indicated in figure 77.

This must be done carefully in order for Sidney to shake down the track. Sidney shakes down the track on the projecting wisps of hair from the sides of his head. If these are too wide, Sidney will not shake;

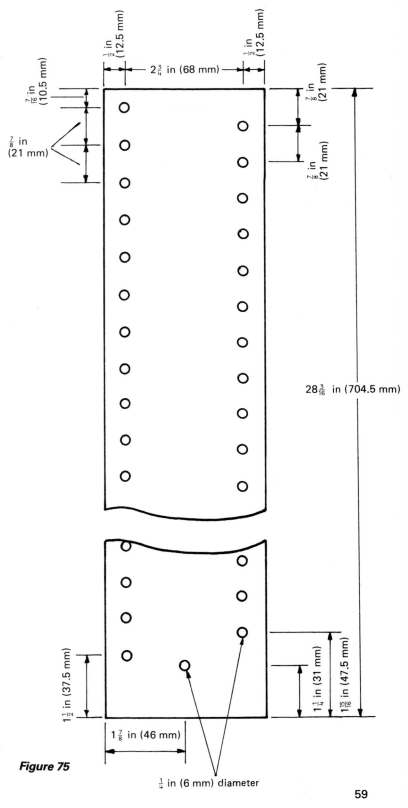

Figure 75

59

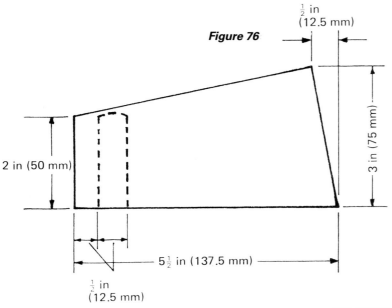

Figure 76

$\frac{1}{2}$ in
(12.5 mm)

2 in (50 mm)

3 in (75 mm)

5$\frac{1}{2}$ in (137.5 mm)

$\frac{1}{2}$ in
(12.5 mm)

on the other hand, if they are too narrow, he will fall straight down the track between the dowels. Cut out Sidney using a coping saw or fret saw. You can now check if Sidney will shake his way down the track. If his performance is good, clean him up neatly with glasspaper and paint a suitable figure on him using bright colours. The stand and track are given two or three coats of varnish after cleaning up, and Sidney is ready to shake.

Figure 77

mark out grid in $\frac{1}{2}$ in
(12.5 mm) squares

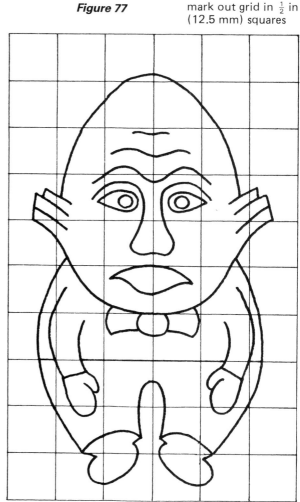

15. Acrobatic Clown

Materials

Body: 1 off 3¾ × 1¾ × ⅜ in (93 × 43 × 9 mm) birch plywood

Arms: 2 off 3½ × 1¼ × ⅛ in (87.5 × 31 × 3 mm) birch plywood

Legs: 2 off 3½ × 1¼ × ⅛ in (87.5 × 31 × 3 mm) birch plywood

Side supports: 2 off 18 × 1¼ × ⅜ in (450 × 31 × 9 mm) hardwood

Cross bar: 1 off 2½ × 1¼ × ¾ in (62.5 × 31 × 18 mm) hardwood

Hand spacers: 2 off 1 × ¼ in (25 × 6 mm) polythene tube

4 off 1 in (25 mm) no. 8 round-head brass screws

20 in (500 mm) good-quality twine

enamel paint

varnish

Tools

tenon saw
fret saw
coping saw
hand drill
¹⁄₁₆ in (1.5 mm) drill
³⁄₃₂ in (2.25 mm) drill
⅛ in (3 mm) drill
half-round smooth file
screwdriver
cork rubber
glasspaper

Squeeze the handles and the clown will somersault. With practice you can make the clown go through a repertoire of acrobatic feats — swinging, turning and balancing. This toy is difficult to put down, which is why its popularity has remained as strong as ever over the years.

Using the basic format of the clown's

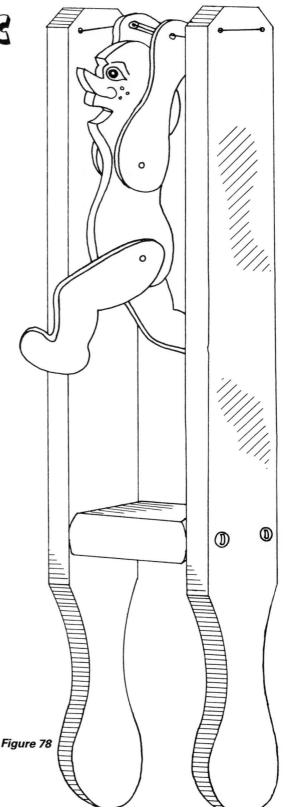

Figure 78

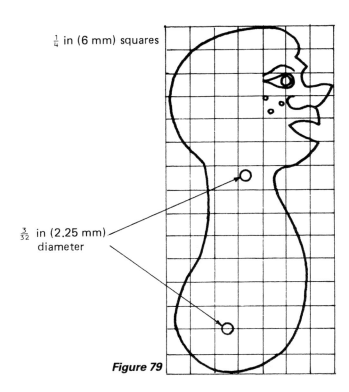

Figure 79

$\frac{1}{4}$ in (6 mm) squares

$\frac{3}{32}$ in (2.25 mm) diameter

body, a whole host of other figures could be made, such as a footballer, painted to represent a particular team, an ice skater or an athlete.

Body

To make the clown's body, you will need a piece of birch plywood 3¾ × 1¾ × ⅜ in (93 × 43 × 9 mm). Mark it out in ¼ in (6 mm) squares as shown in figure 79. Then, using the squares as a guide, mark out the shape of the clown's body onto the plywood. Mark out the two centres and drill with a ³⁄₃₂ in (2.25 mm) drill. These holes will be used later to join the arms and legs to the body of the clown. Cut out the body carefully using a fret saw to avoid chipping the plywood. If the plywood does chip, you will need to use a wood filler to obtain the final finish.

Arms and legs

Two pieces of birch plywood 3½ × 1¼ × ⅛ in (87.5 × 31 × 3 mm) will be required for the arms, and two pieces of the same size of birch plywood for the legs. Mark out all

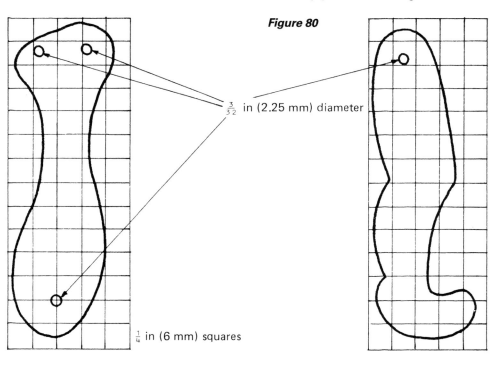

Figure 80

$\frac{3}{32}$ in (2.25 mm) diameter

$\frac{1}{4}$ in (6 mm) squares

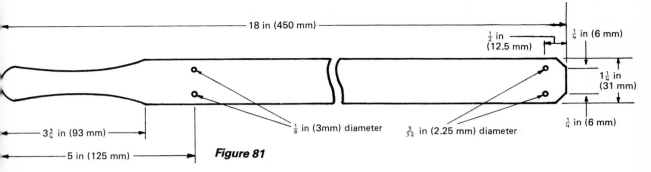

18 in (450 mm)

$\frac{1}{2}$ in (12.5 mm)

$\frac{1}{4}$ in (6 mm)

$1\frac{1}{4}$ in (31 mm)

$\frac{1}{4}$ in (6 mm)

$3\frac{3}{4}$ in (93 mm)

5 in (125 mm)

$\frac{1}{8}$ in (3mm) diameter

$\frac{3}{32}$ in (2.25 mm) diameter

Figure 81

four pieces into ¼ in (6 mm) squares and carefully transfer the shapes from figure 80 onto your work. Mark out the centres for drilling on the arms and legs and drill the holes ³⁄₃₂ in (2.25 mm) in diameter. Cut out the shapes with the fret saw and clean up the arms and legs, together with the body. Lightly round all edges to give a good finish. Next paint the body in appropriate colours; while you are waiting for them to dry, the other parts can be made.

Side supports

The side supports look attractive if they are made from hardwood. For this purpose you will need two pieces 18 × 1¼ × ³⁄₈ in (450 × 31 × 9 mm). Mark them out to the dimensions given in figure 81 and drill both sets of holes as shown. Shape the handles to suit and cut them out with a coping saw or fret saw.

Cross bar

The cross bar is made from a piece of hardwood 2½ × 1¼ × ¾ in (62.5 × 31 × 18 mm). Very lightly round the ends as shown in figure 82. Then lightly radius all edges of the side supports and cross bar and finish with glasspaper ready for varnishing.

When the side supports and cross bar have been varnished, screw them together using four 1 in (25 mm) no. 8 round-head brass screws. To do this, place the cross bar in position (figure 83)

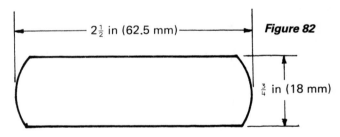

2½ in (62.5 mm)

$\frac{3}{4}$ in (18 mm)

Figure 82

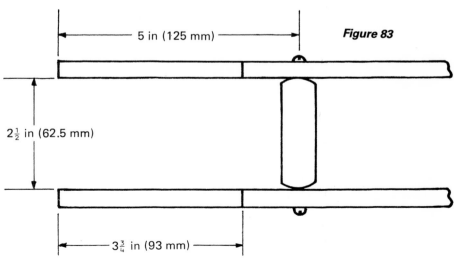

5 in (125 mm)

Figure 83

2½ in (62.5 mm)

3¾ in (93 mm)

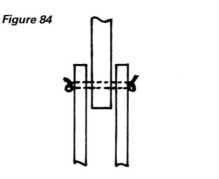

Figure 84

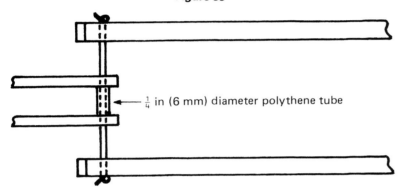

Figure 85

$\frac{1}{4}$ in (6 mm) diameter polythene tube

and, using the ⅛ in (3 mm) holes in the side supports as a guide, drill into the cross bar using a 1/16 in (1.5 mm) diameter drill in preparation for the screws. Make sure that the screws are tightened sufficiently to allow obvious movement at the top of the side supports when the handles are squeezed.

Final assembly

Using a good-quality twine, assemble the body as shown in figure 84, knotting the ends so that the joints move freely but not loosely. When the clown is complete, lay him face down with his arms above his head, so that his hands point into the top of the assembled side supports and line up with the holes in the end of the side supports. Before threading the twine, cut two pieces 1 in (25 mm) long of ¼ in (6 mm) diameter polythene tube, which will act as spacers between the clown's hands (figure 85). Pick up the toy by the handles; as the clown falls down, the string will automatically cross so that it is ready for working.

16. Somersaulting Man

Materials

Side supports: 2 off 27⅛ × ½ × ½ in (678 × 12.5 × 12.5 mm) softwood
Rungs: 9 off 3 × ⅜ × ⅛ in (75 × 9 × 3 mm) birch plywood
Base: 2 off 4 × 4 × ¾ in (100 × 100 × 18 mm) softwood
Man: 1 off 3½ × 1¼ × ¾ in (87.5 × 31 × 18 mm) softwood
Template: 1 off 3½ × 2½ × ¼ in (87.5 × 62.5 × 6 mm) birch plywood
18 off ½ in (12.5 mm) veneer pins
adhesive
enamel paint
varnish

Tools

tenon saw
hand drill
⅜ in (9 mm) drill
½ in (12.5 mm) drill
½ in (12.5 mm) chisel
mallet
hammer
jack plane or half-round smooth file
cork rubber
glasspaper

The man is trapped on the ladder to somersault perpetually from top to bottom. Turn the ladder upside down to make him start his never-ending journey once again.

Ladder

For the rungs of the ladder you will need nine pieces of 3 × ⅜ × ⅛ in (75 × 9 × 3 mm) birch plywood. Cut these to length and round the edges of the rungs with

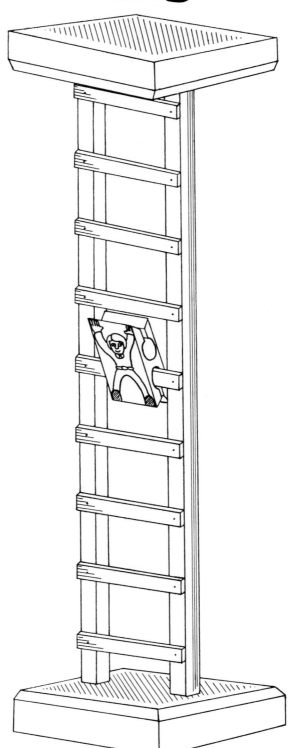

Figure 86

65

glasspaper, so that they will fit and rotate in a ⅜ in (9 mm) diameter hole as shown in figure 87. For the ladder you will need two side posts of 27⅛ × ½ × ½ in (678 × 12.5 × 12.5 mm) softwood. Saw these to the lengths given and lightly radius the corners of the posts during the cleaning-up process.

Before the rungs are fitted to the side supports to make the ladder, it is a good idea to make a template, so that each rung is accurately spaced up the side supports. Accuracy is essential for this model, so that the man will somersault smoothly down the ladder. The template is made from a piece of plywood 3½ × 2½ × ¼ in (87.5 × 62.5 × 6 mm) and is used as shown in figure 88.

Carefully mark out the position for the first rung. Position the side supports and apply a spot of glue to each end of the rung. Fit the rung in position using a ½ in (12.5 mm) veneer pin as indicated. Position the template and fit the additional rungs as explained above. It is a good idea to turn the template around and not over as each additional rung is fitted in position. This helps to stop any minor inaccuracies that may be present in the template; over the length of the ladder these would be magnified quite considerably. As each rung is fitted, it is advisable to clean off any surplus glue which may have squeezed out when the rung was nailed into position.

For the base of the ladder you will require two pieces of softwood 4 × 4 × ¾ in (100 × 100 × 18 mm). Mark out the two pieces as shown in figure 89 on both sides of each piece. Using a ½ in (12.5 mm) drill, drill out the centre of each ½ in (12.5 mm) square right through the base. Cut out the rest of the waste using a ½ in (12.5 mm) chisel and mallet, cutting across the grain. Check that the side supports of the ladder fit in, and if necessary ease the joint.

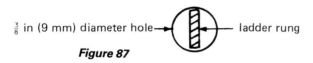

⅜ in (9 mm) diameter hole → ← ladder rung

Figure 87

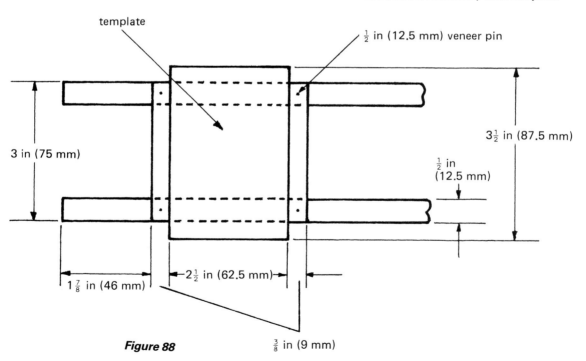

template

½ in (12.5 mm) veneer pin

3 in (75 mm)

3½ in (87.5 mm)

½ in (12.5 mm)

1⅞ in (46 mm)

2½ in (62.5 mm)

Figure 88

⅜ in (9 mm)

Finish the top edges of the base with a ¼ in (6 mm) chamfer, for which you will need a plane. If this is not available, radius them with a half-round smooth file. Do not glue the base to the side supports at this stage, as the somersaulting man must be on the ladder before the bases are attached.

Somersaulting man

The somersaulting man is made from a piece of softwood 3½ x 1¼ x ¾ in (87.5 x 31 x 18 mm). Mark it out as shown in figure 90. Drill the two centres with a ⅜ in (9 mm) diameter drill and cut out the slots to fit the rungs, which are ⅛ in (3 mm) wide. To make the slots, place the work in a vice and carefully cut out the slots with a tenon saw. The man will only work properly if this operation is done accurately.

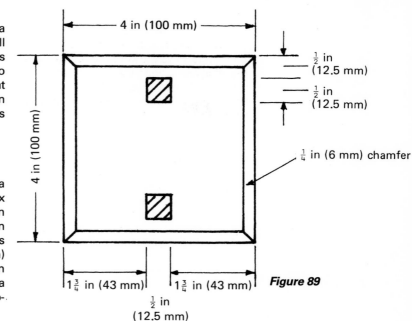

Figure 89

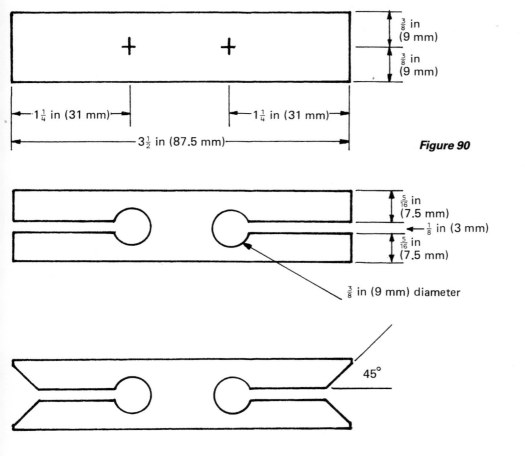

Figure 90

Finally, cut the two ends with the tenon saw to an angle of 45° as shown. Check at this stage to see if the slots will fit the rungs of the ladder; if they are too tight, wrap a piece of medium glasspaper around a steel rule and enlarge the slots until a good fit on the rung of the ladder is obtained. The width of the slot must just allow a smooth fit on the rung. If the slot is too wide, it will not guide the man accurately to the next rung when he is somersaulting, and instead he will miss the rung and drop off the ladder. If this happens you will have to start again and make another man.

Check the man on the ladder and when you are satisfied with his somersaulting performance, clean him up ready for painting. You may prefer to paint his shape either directly onto the wood, or onto a piece of paper which can then be glued onto the wood (figure 91).

Finishing

Before assembling the ladder with the somersaulting man on it, the ladder and base can be finished with a thin coat of a brightly coloured stained varnish. When dry, carefully flat the finish down with flourpaper, so that any build up of varnish is removed and does not spoil the movement of the man down the ladder. Position the man on the ladder and glue the two bases in position.

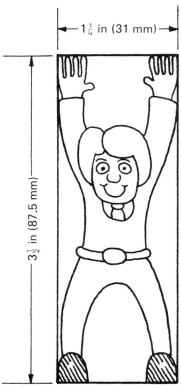

Figure 91

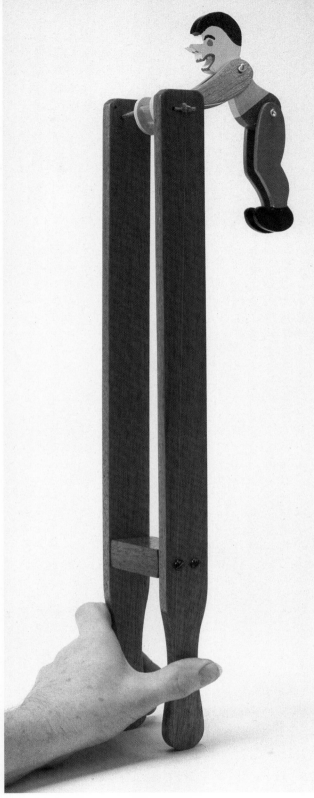

Acrobatic Clown

Performing Monkey

Boomerang

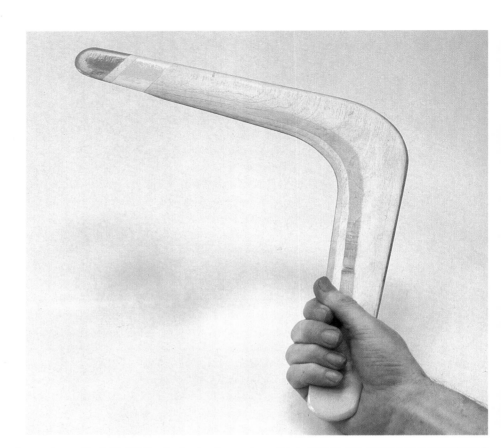

Submarine

17. Performing Monkey

Materials

Body: 1 off 3¾ × 2¼ × ⅜ in (93 × 56 × 9 mm) birch plywood

Arms: 2 off 3 × ¾ × ¼ in (75 × 18 × 6 mm) birch plywood

Legs: 2 off 3¼ × 1¼ × ¼ in (81 × 31 × 6 mm) birch plywood

Base: 1 off 4 × 4 × ⅞ in (100 × 100 × 21 mm) hardwood

Vertical rod: 1 off 20 × ⅜ in (500 × 9 mm) dowel

Sliding block: 1 off 1¾ × 1½ × ⅞ in (43 × 37.5 × 21 mm) hardwood

Moving rod: 1 off 10 × ⅜ in (250 × 9 mm) dowel

20 in (500 mm) good-quality twine

enamel paint

varnish

Tools

tenon saw

fret saw

hand drill

³⁄₃₂ in (2.25 mm) drill

⅜ in (9 mm) drill

¹³⁄₃₂ in (9.75 mm) drill or ⅜ in (9 mm) drill

jack plane or half-round smooth file

cork rubber

glasspaper

This colourful monkey has been a favourite with children for many generations. He will delight you with the variety of poses and postures which he will perform as you change the position of the moving rod. When he is not being used you can select a posture which he will retain and he will make an interesting ornament that can be changed at will. This toy is seldom seen now and I find that it becomes a talk-

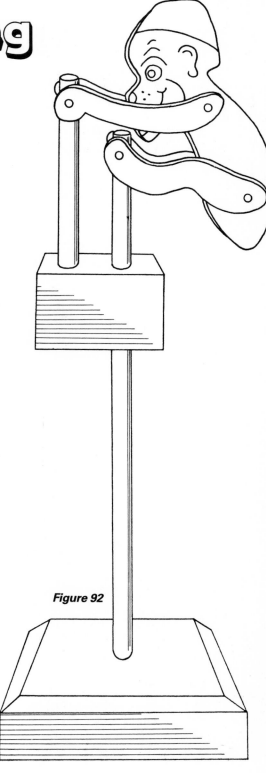

Figure 92

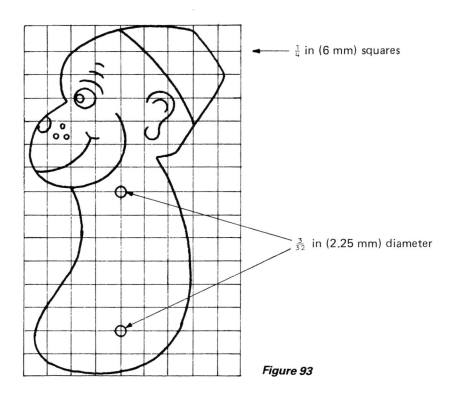

$\frac{1}{4}$ in (6 mm) squares

$\frac{3}{32}$ in (2.25 mm) diameter

Figure 93

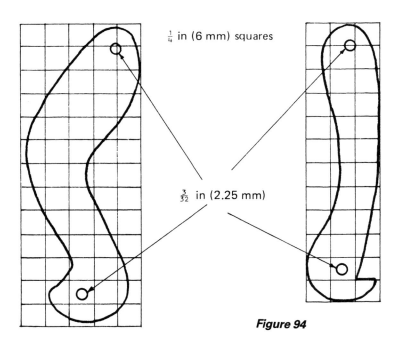

$\frac{1}{4}$ in (6 mm) squares

$\frac{3}{32}$ in (2.25 mm)

Figure 94

ing point; everyone, whatever their age, wants to 'have a go'.

Body

To make your performing monkey you will need a piece of birch plywood 3¾ × 2¼ × ⅜ in (93 × 56 × 9 mm). Mark it out in ¼ in (6 mm) squares as shown in figure 93 and, using the squares as a guide, mark out the outline of the monkey's body. The detail shown is a suggestion for painting the monkey when you have finished him.

Next mark out the two centres and drill with a ³⁄₃₂ in (2.25 mm) drill. These holes will be used later for joining the arms and legs to the body of the monkey so that a completed monkey will move realistically. The body is cut out using a fret saw. Do this carefully and do not try to hurry it, otherwise you may chip the outer veneers of the ply and spoil the finished item.

Arms and legs

For the arms you will need two pieces of 3 × ¾ × ¼ in (75 × 18 × 6 mm) birch plywood, and for the legs you will need two pieces of 3¼ × 1¼ × ¼ in (81 × 31 × 6 mm) birch plywood. Mark out all four pieces into ¼ in (6 mm) squares and carefully draw on the shapes of the arms and the legs as in figure 94. Mark out the centres of the arms and legs and drill the holes ³⁄₃₂ in (2.25 mm) in diameter. Carefully cut to shape with a fret saw.

At this stage, clean up the body, arms and legs and lightly round the edges with glasspaper. You are now ready to paint them in the colours you have chosen. While you are waiting for the paint to dry, you can proceed with the next part of the toy.

Base and vertical rod

The base is made from a block of 4 × 4 × ⅞ in (100 × 100 × 21 mm) hardwood. Find the centre of the block using diagonals, then drill a hole right through the centre with a ⅜ in (9 mm) diameter drill. If a plane is available give the edges a ¼ in (6 mm) chamfer; if not, round the edges with a

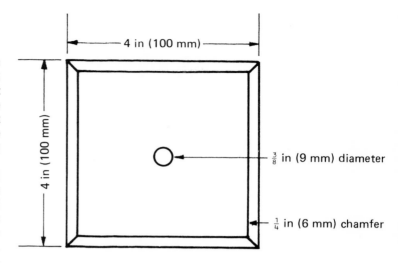

⅜ in (9 mm) diameter

¼ in (6 mm) chamfer

Figure 95

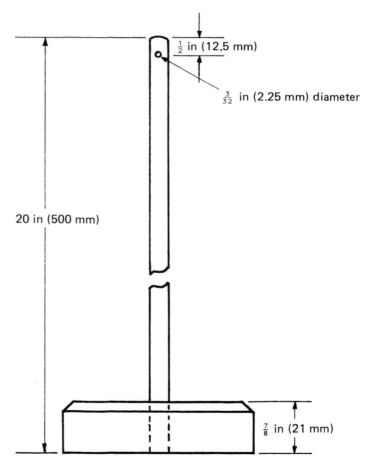

½ in (12.5 mm)

³⁄₃₂ in (2.25 mm) diameter

20 in (500 mm)

⅞ in (21 mm)

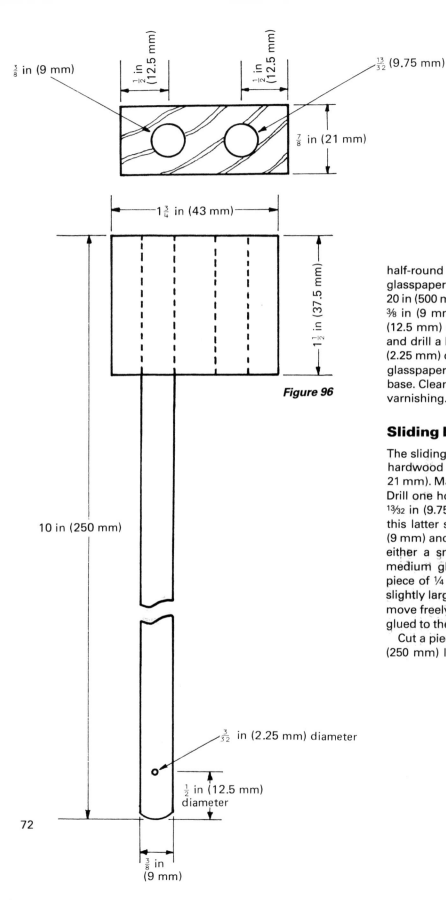

$\frac{3}{8}$ in (9 mm)

$\frac{1}{2}$ in (12.5 mm)

$\frac{1}{2}$ in (12.5 mm)

$\frac{13}{32}$ (9.75 mm)

$\frac{7}{8}$ in (21 mm)

$1\frac{3}{4}$ in (43 mm)

$1\frac{1}{2}$ in (37.5 mm)

Figure 96

10 in (250 mm)

$\frac{3}{32}$ in (2.25 mm) diameter

$\frac{1}{2}$ in (12.5 mm) diameter

$\frac{3}{8}$ in (9 mm)

half-round smooth file and finish with glasspaper (figure 95). Cut the vertical rod 20 in (500 mm) long from a piece of dowel $\frac{3}{8}$ in (9 mm) in diameter. Measure $\frac{1}{2}$ in (12.5 mm) down from the top of the rod and drill a hole in the centre with a $\frac{3}{32}$ in (2.25 mm) drill. Lightly dome the top with glasspaper and then glue the rod into the base. Clean up with glasspaper, ready for varnishing.

Sliding block and moving rod

The sliding block is made from a piece of hardwood $1\frac{3}{4} \times 1\frac{1}{2} \times \frac{7}{8}$ in (43 × 37.5 × 21 mm). Mark it out as shown in figure 96. Drill one hole $\frac{3}{8}$ in (9 mm) and the other $\frac{13}{32}$ in (9.75 mm) in diameter. If a drill of this latter size is not available, drill $\frac{3}{8}$ in (9 mm) and slightly enlarge the hole with either a small round file or a piece of medium glasspaper wrapped around a piece of $\frac{1}{4}$ in (6 mm) dowel. One hole is slightly larger than the other so that it will move freely up and down the vertical rod glued to the base.

Cut a piece of $\frac{3}{8}$ in (9 mm) dowel, 10 in (250 mm) long, for the moving rod, and

72

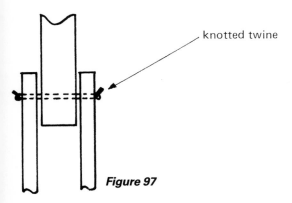

knotted twine

Figure 97

measure in ½ in (12.5 mm) from one end. Drill a hole in the centre $^{3}/_{32}$ in (2.25 mm) in diameter. Dome this end lightly with glasspaper and glue the other end into the $^{3}/_{8}$ in (9 mm) diameter hole in the block. Lightly radius all edges to the block with glasspaper and finish the assembly with glasspaper ready for varnishing.

After varnishing, assemble the sliding block onto the main upright and check for free movement. It may be necessary after varnishing slightly to enlarge the $^{13}/_{32}$ in (9.75 mm) diameter hole to obtain a smooth movement.

Final assembly

Assemble the joints of the body using a good-quality twine and knot the ends as in figure 97, so that the joints can move freely without being too loose. After this, join the feet of the monkey to the fixed upright and attach the hands to the moving upright, again using strong twine and knotting the ends. The monkey will now perform for you as you move the sliding block up and down.

18. Pecking Bird

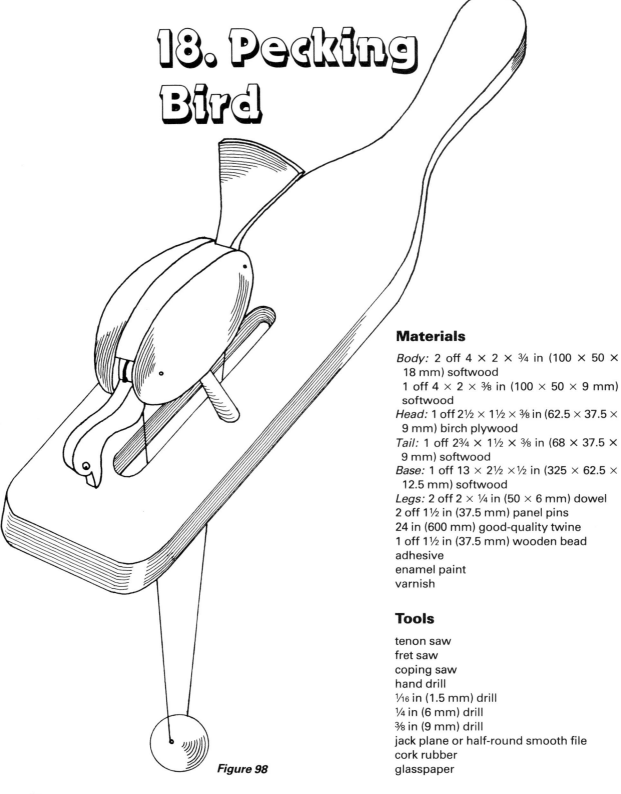

Figure 98

Materials

Body: 2 off 4 × 2 × ¾ in (100 × 50 × 18 mm) softwood
1 off 4 × 2 × ⅜ in (100 × 50 × 9 mm) softwood
Head: 1 off 2½ × 1½ × ⅜ in (62.5 × 37.5 × 9 mm) birch plywood
Tail: 1 off 2¾ × 1½ × ⅜ in (68 × 37.5 × 9 mm) softwood
Base: 1 off 13 × 2½ × ½ in (325 × 62.5 × 12.5 mm) softwood
Legs: 2 off 2 × ¼ in (50 × 6 mm) dowel
2 off 1½ in (37.5 mm) panel pins
24 in (600 mm) good-quality twine
1 off 1½ in (37.5 mm) wooden bead
adhesive
enamel paint
varnish

Tools

tenon saw
fret saw
coping saw
hand drill
1/16 in (1.5 mm) drill
¼ in (6 mm) drill
⅜ in (9 mm) drill
jack plane or half-round smooth file
cork rubber
glasspaper

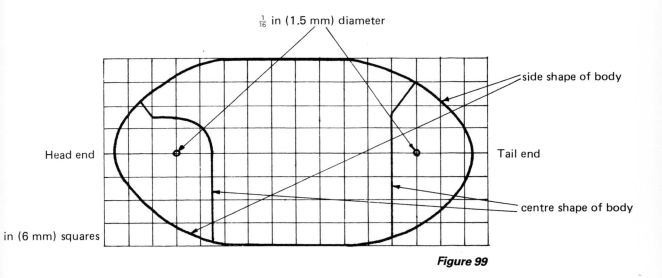

$\frac{1}{16}$ in (1.5 mm) diameter

side shape of body

Head end

Tail end

centre shape of body

in (6 mm) squares

Figure 99

Hold the handle of this toy and swing the weight gently backwards and forwards like a pendulum to make the head and the tail rise and fall alternately, giving the impression that the bird is pecking. This toy will appeal most to the younger child, but the older child will find it very satisfying to make. With a little experimentation, other birds and animals could be made using this method.

Body

The bird's body is laminated from three pieces of softwood. For the two outer parts you will need two pieces 4 × 2 × ¾ in (100 × 50 × 18 mm) and for the centre part a piece 4 × 2 × ⅜ in (100 × 50 × 9 mm). Mark out these pieces in ¼ in (6 mm) squares, then mark out the centre piece onto the squares to the required shape (figure 99).

Cut the centre piece to shape using a coping saw. Then glue it in position between the two outer sides of the bird's body. When the glue has set, transfer the body side shape onto the work. Mark in the two pivot holes and drill these 1⁄16 in (1.5 mm) in diameter.

Cut the body shape using the coping

saw. If you are keen for your bird to have a realistic appearance, shape the body to resemble an egg: use a rough file to gain the required shape, and then glasspaper through the grades to a smooth finish. If you feel this is too much work, the body can be left to the sawn shape with just the edges lightly radiused and then glasspapered to a good finish ready for painting.

Head

For the head you will need a piece of birch plywood 2½ × 1½ × ⅜ in (62.5 × 37.5 × 9 mm). Rule it out into ¼ in (6 mm) squares, then mark out the shape from figure 100 onto your plywood. Drill the pivot hole 1⁄16 in (1.5 mm) in diameter and also a hole 1⁄16 in (1.5 mm) in diameter down through the neck to take the string (figure 100). Using a coping saw, carefully cut out the shape of the head. Clean up the edges and lightly radius the corners to a good finish. Before painting the head, check that it slots into the body and slides up and down freely. It does not need to be too loose, as long as a free movement up and down is obtained.

Using a 1½ in (37.5 mm) panel pin, line up the pivot holes of the body and the

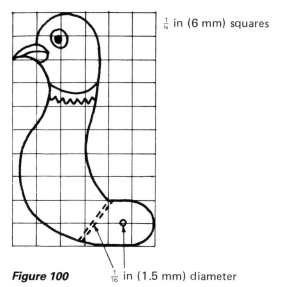

$\frac{1}{4}$ in (6 mm) squares

Figure 100 $\frac{1}{16}$ in (1.5 mm) diameter

to shape using a tenon saw or coping saw. After cutting out, taper the tail to the dimensions shown in the drawing and round the end. This can be done with a plane, or, if one is not available, a half-round smooth file. Drill the $\frac{1}{16}$ in (1.5 mm) diameter pivot hole and also the $\frac{1}{16}$ in (1.5 mm) diameter hole for the string (figure 101). Fit the tail into the body and check for free movement. When this is satisfactory, line up the pivot holes and insert another 1½ in (37.5 mm) panel pin into the body and tail, checking for a smooth movement. Mark the panel pin to size, remove it and cut to size. Clean up the tail to a smooth finish with glasspaper in preparation for painting.

head, insert the panel pin and check that the head will pivot up and down with the panel pin in position. Mark the panel pin to size, remove it, cut it to size using a junior hacksaw, and file for a fit flush with the bird's body.

Tail

The tail is made from a piece of softwood 2¾ × 1½ × ⅜ in (68 × 37.5 × 9 mm). Mark out the tail as shown in figure 101 and cut

Base

The base is made from a piece of softwood 13 × 2½ × ½ in (325 × 62.5 × 12.5 mm). Mark it out as shown in figure 102. Cut out the handle with a coping saw and, if necessary, file to a finished shape with a half-round smooth file. Mark out the slot, drill out each end with a ⅜ in (9 mm) diameter drill and remove the waste wood with a coping saw. Clean up the slot with a half-round smooth file and glasspaper to a smooth finish. File and glasspaper the two corners at the front of the base to a neat radius.

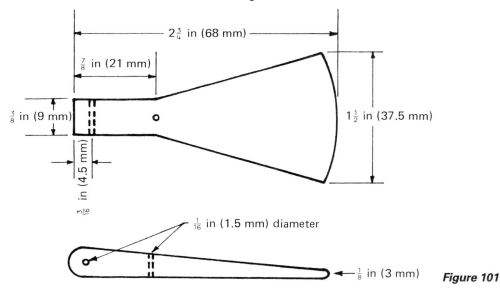

2¾ in (68 mm)

⅞ in (21 mm)

⅜ in (9 mm)

$\frac{3}{16}$ in (4.5 mm)

1½ in (37.5 mm)

$\frac{1}{16}$ in (1.5 mm) diameter

$\frac{1}{8}$ in (3 mm)   **Figure 101**

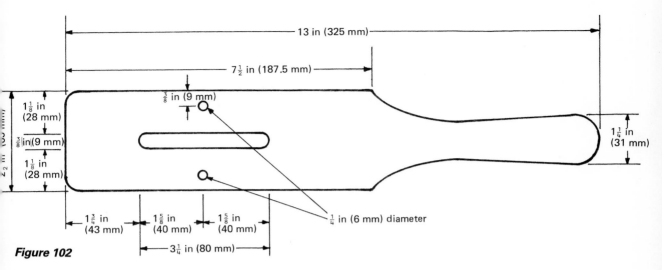

Figure 102

Drill the two ¼ in (6 mm) holes for the legs at a slight angle as indicated in figure 103, then clean up the base ready for painting or varnishing.

Legs

The legs are made from two pieces of dowel 2 × ¼ in (50 × 6 mm); before fitting them, it is necessary to drill two ¼ in (6 mm) holes in the centre along the side of the bird's body.

Final assembly

When the body and base have been painted or varnished according to your choice, glue and assemble the body to the base. Take a piece of good-quality twine 24 in (600 mm) long and thread it through the head, knotting it underneath. Take the thread through the slot in the base and thread on a 1½ in (37.5 mm) wooden bead or other suitable weight. Then bring the thread back through the slot before passing it through the tail and knotting neatly underneath (figure 104).

Hold the base horizontally, and check that the weight hangs centrally when the bird's head is up and the tail down. Holding this position, apply a spot of glue to the twine and bead so that the bead keeps in its place. All that remains now is to swing the weight backwards and forwards, and your bird will peck.

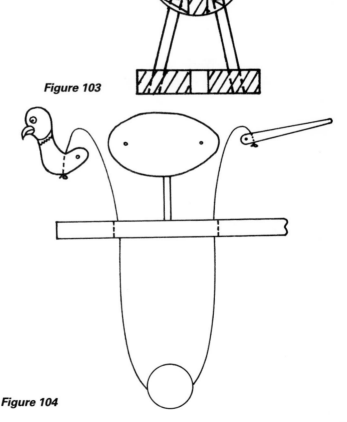

Figure 103

Figure 104

19. Dancing Ballerina

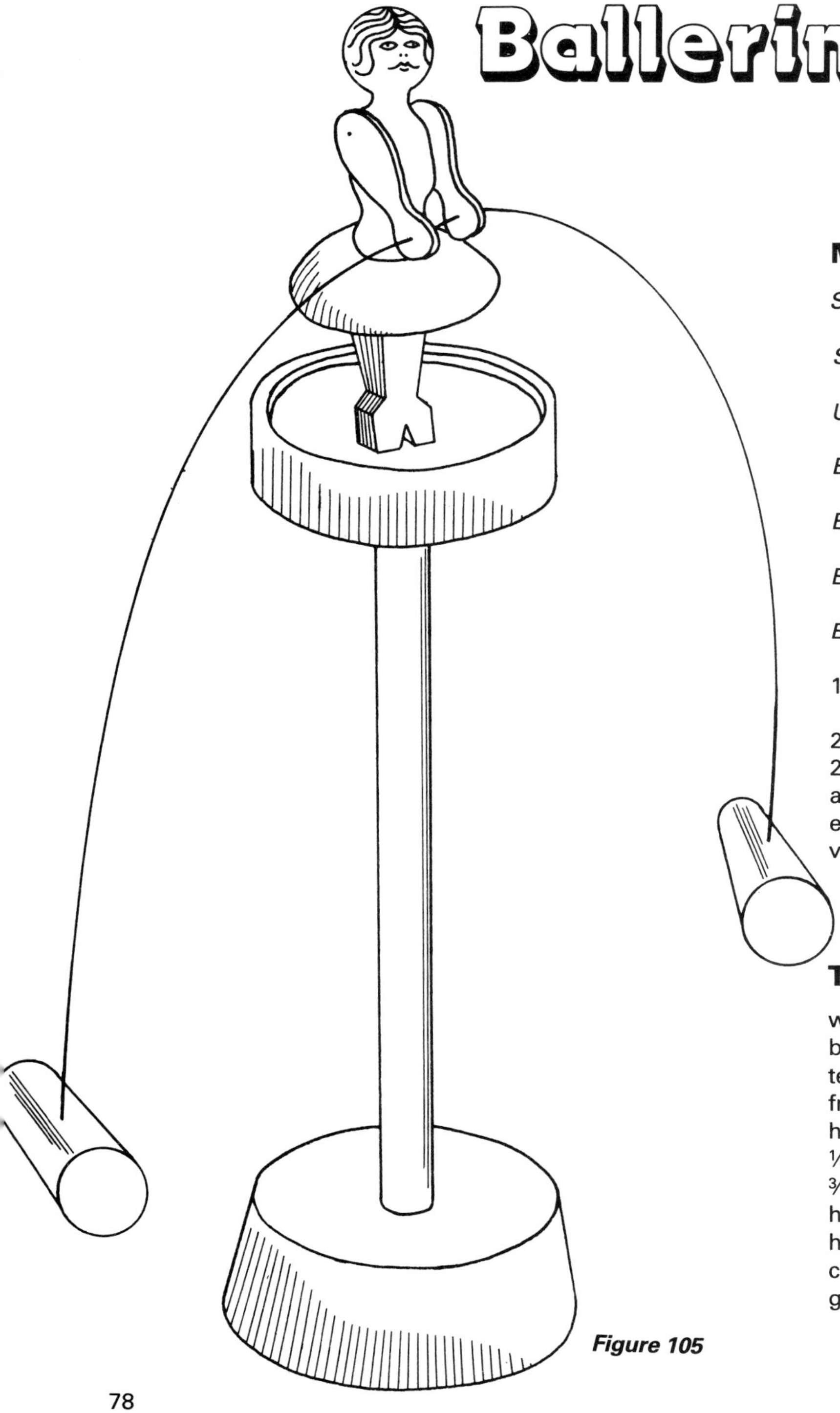

Figure 105

Materials

Stand top: 1 off 3½ × 3½ × 1 in (87.5 × 87.5 × 25 mm) hardwood

Stand base: 1 off 3¾ × 3¾ × 1⅛ in (93 × 93 × 28 mm) hardwood

Upright: 1 off 10 × ⅜ in (250 × 9 mm) dowel

Ballerina body: 1 off 3¾ × 1 × 1 in (93 × 25 × 25 mm) hardwood

Ballerina skirt: 1 off 2¼ × 2¼ × ⅜ in (56 × 56 × 9 mm) hardwood

Ballerina arms: 2 off 1½ × ½ × ⅛ in (37.5 × 12.5 × 3 mm) plywood

Balancing weights: 2 off 2 × ⅞ in (50 × 21 mm) hardwood

1 off 24 in (600 mm) x ⅛ in (3 mm) (approximately) cane

2 off ½ in (12.5 mm) panel pins

20 in (500 mm) twine

adhesive

enamel paint

varnish

Tools

woodworker's lathe
basic turning tools
tenon saw
fret saw
hand drill
⅛ in (3 mm) drill (or to suit cane)
⅜ in (9 mm) drill
hammer
half-round smooth file
cork rubber
glasspaper

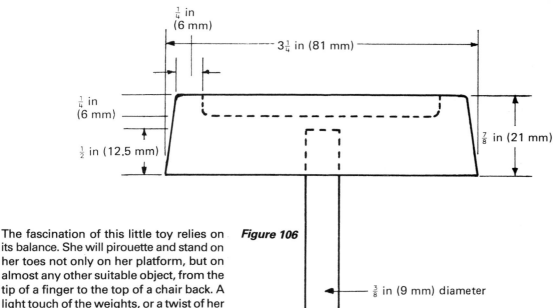

$\frac{1}{4}$ in
(6 mm)

$3\frac{1}{4}$ in (81 mm)

$\frac{1}{4}$ in
(6 mm)

$\frac{1}{2}$ in (12.5 mm)

$\frac{7}{8}$ in (21 mm)

Figure 106

$\frac{3}{8}$ in (9 mm) diameter

The fascination of this little toy relies on its balance. She will pirouette and stand on her toes not only on her platform, but on almost any other suitable object, from the tip of a finger to the top of a chair back. A light touch of the weights, or a twist of her body, will set her in motion and she will sway and twirl, performing her repertoire for you. She will also become a tightrope walker. She will move from one end of a tautly held piece of string to the other if the string is lowered slightly, apparently defying the laws of nature, and amazing you with her balancing skill. To make this toy you will need to have access to a woodturning lathe and a knowledge of the basic techniques involved in wood turning.

Stand

The top of the stand is turned from a piece of hardwood 3½ × 3½ × 1 in (87.5 × 87.5 × 25 mm). Find the centre by drawing diagonals, and counterbore with a drill of suitable size to fit the screw of the screw-flange chuck, in preparation for mounting on the chuck. It is important, when counterboring the top piece, that both the counterbored hole and the screw of the chuck do not penetrate into the base deeper than ½ in (12.5 mm); otherwise a hole might appear in the centre of the top, which would affect the performance of the dancing ballerina. If the screw of the screw-flange chuck is longer than ½ in (12.5 mm) and cannot be adjusted, then you will have to mount the top using a suitable thickness of plywood backing to

prevent the screw point coming through the surface when the recess is turned in the top.

When the top has been mounted satisfactorily onto the screw-flange chuck, turn the top to the dimensions given in figure 106. While the top is on the chuck, glasspaper through the grades to a smooth finish. Remove the top from the chuck and drill a ⅜ in (9 mm) diameter hole in the centre to a depth of ½ in (12.5 mm).

For the base of the stand you will need a piece of hardwood 3¾ × 3¾ × 1⅛ in (93 × 93 × 28 mm). Draw diagonals from the corners on the underside of the base to find the centre. Counterbore this, and then mount the base on the chuck. Turn the base to the dimensions shown in figure 107. Glasspaper the base through the grades to a smooth finish. Remove the base from the chuck and then drill in the centre through the base with a ⅜ in (9 mm) diameter drill.

For the upright you will need a piece of 10 × ⅜ in (250 × 9 mm) dowel. Clean the dowel with glasspaper, apply glue to the top and bottom and assemble the stand. When the stand is assembled, apply two or three coats of clear varnish to give a good finish.

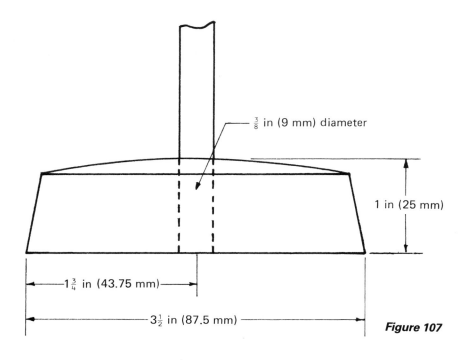

$\frac{3}{8}$ in (9 mm) diameter

1 in (25 mm)

1$\frac{3}{4}$ in (43.75 mm)

3$\frac{1}{2}$ in (87.5 mm)

Figure 107

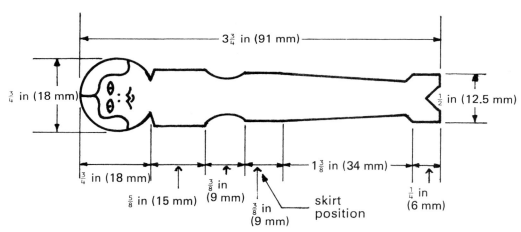

3$\frac{3}{4}$ in (91 mm)

$\frac{3}{4}$ in (18 mm)

$\frac{1}{2}$ in (12.5 mm)

$\frac{3}{4}$ in (18 mm)

$\frac{5}{8}$ in (15 mm)

$\frac{3}{8}$ in (9 mm)

$\frac{3}{8}$ in (9 mm)

skirt position

1$\frac{3}{8}$ in (34 mm)

$\frac{1}{4}$ in (6 mm)

Figure 108

Figure 109

$\frac{1}{8}$ in (3 mm)

80

Ballerina

The body of the ballerina is turned from a suitable piece of hardwood 3¾ × 1 × 1 in (93 × 25 × 25 mm). You need to allow an extra 1 in (25 mm) on this length so that the work can be mounted on the lathe to be turned between centres. Find the centre by drawing diagonals before mounting the wood between centres on the lathe. Turn the piece of wood down to a diameter of ¾ in (18 mm) and then shape the body as indicated in figure 108. Glasspaper the body to a good finish before removing from the lathe, and with a smooth file remove the waste as shown in figure 109.

Skirt

For the ballerina's skirt, you will need a matching piece of hardwood 2¼ × 2¼ × ⅜ in (56 × 56 × 9 mm). Mount this on the screw-flange chuck and turn to the shape shown in figure 110. Clean up the work with glasspaper and remove from the screw-flange chuck. Drill in the centre with a ½ in (12.5 mm) drill, and slip the skirt into position on the body of the ballerina (figure 108). Glue in place.

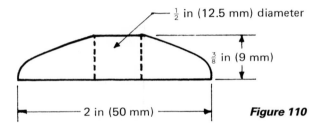

½ in (12.5 mm) diameter

⅜ in (9 mm)

2 in (50 mm)

Figure 110

Arms

For the arms of the ballerina you will need two pieces of plywood 1½ × ½ × ⅛ in (37.5 × 12.5 × 3 mm). Mark these out as shown in figure 111 and carefully cut to shape using a fret saw. Before drilling the hands to receive the balancing cane, drill a piece of scrap wood to check that the size of the drill is suitable; the cane must form a tight fit in the hands in order to achieve a correct balance between the weights and the body, so that the ballerina can perform. If a loose fit occurs it will be extremely difficult to achieve the correct balance and it may be necessary to make new arms. A suitable thickness of cane is approximately ⅛ in (3 mm). The cane is the type used for basketry work, but if this is not available it is possible to use ⅛ in (3 mm) diameter dowel if it is of good quality.

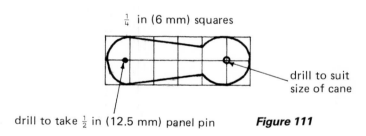

¼ in (6 mm) squares

drill to suit size of cane

drill to take ½ in (12.5 mm) panel pin

Figure 111

When you are satisfied with the fit, carefully drill the hands, and glasspaper to a finish. Pin and glue the arms to the body, so that the hands are resting on the ballerina's skirt. Use two ½ in (12.5 mm) panel pins for this and cut off the ends so that they are approximately ⅜ in (9 mm) long. It is also a good idea to apply a spot of glue to the hands so that they are glued to the skirt. This will help to increase the strength of the toy.

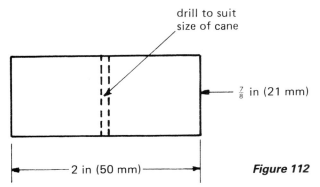

drill to suit
size of cane

$\frac{7}{8}$ in (21 mm)

2 in (50 mm)

Figure 112

Balancing weights

The weights are made from two pieces of hardwood 2 in (50 mm) long and $\frac{7}{8}$ in (21 mm) in diameter. Drill them in the centre to receive the cane. Glasspaper and varnish the weights to a good finish (figure 112). A piece of cane 24 in (600 mm) long is required to support the weights. Soak the cane in water until it becomes pliable and then bend the cane, so that the two ends are approximately 14 in (350 mm) apart. Tie these in position and leave the cane overnight to dry. When the string is removed, the cane should retain its shape.

Thread the cane through the hands of the ballerina so that an equal amount of cane extends on either side of the hands. Then glue the weights in position on each end of the cane. Turn the hands on the cane until the weights are hanging in the correct position to make the ballerina stand upright on her stand. This adjustment is critical and it will need some care to achieve the delicate balance between the weights and the ballerina, to make her perform properly. Apply glue to both sides of the hands and the cane. Make sure that the glue has thoroughly hardened before you attempt to set her dancing.

Finishing

The model is considerably improved if a face and hair are painted on the ballerina and her dress is also painted.

20. Whipping and Spinning Tops

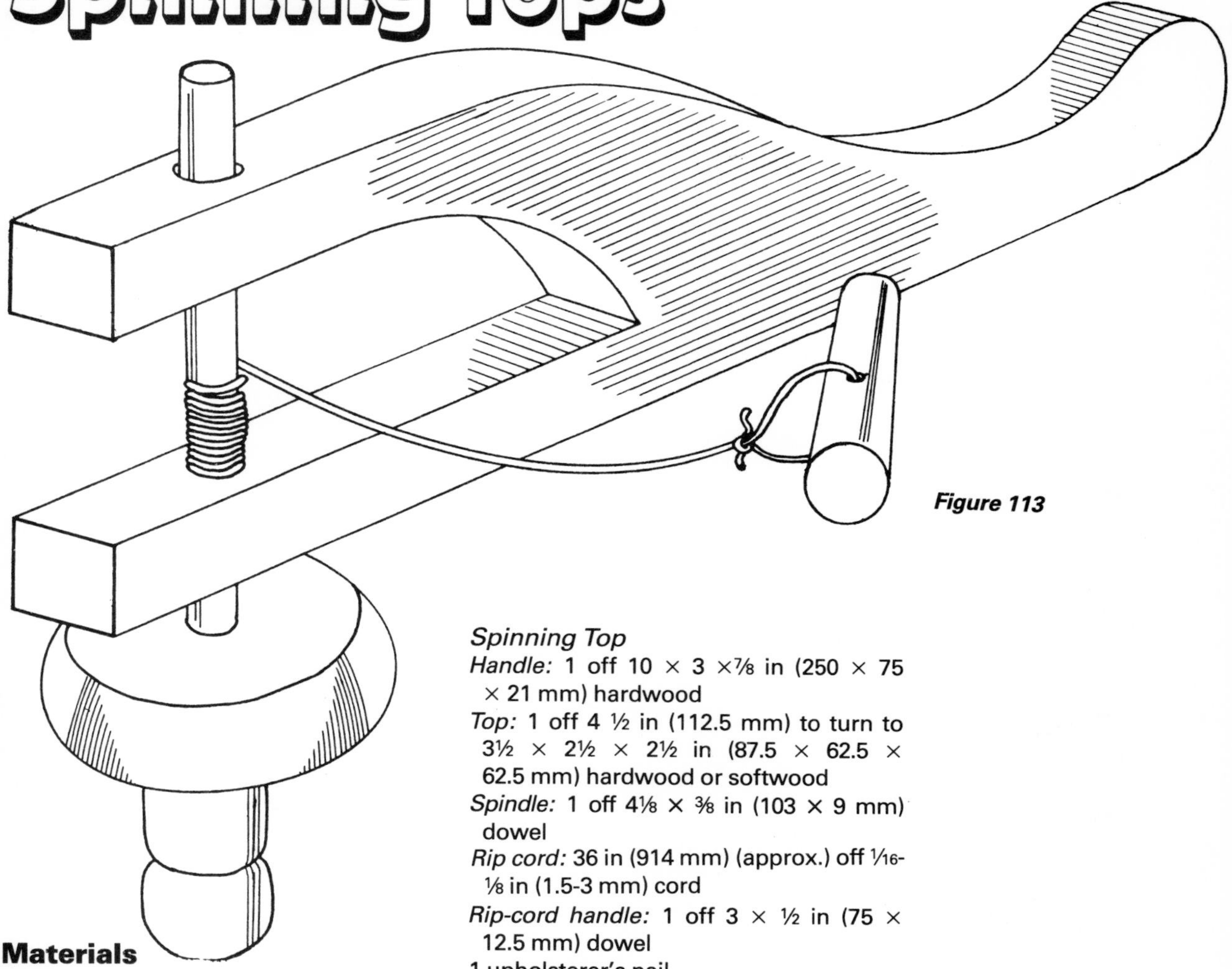

Figure 113

Materials

Whipping top

Top: 1 off 4 ½ in (112.5 mm) to turn to 3½ × 2 × 2 in (87.5 × 50 × 50 mm) hardwood or softwood

Whip: 1 off 20 × ½ in (500 × 12.5 mm) dowel

36 in (914 mm) (approx.) off ³⁄₃₂ in (2.25 mm) cord

1 upholsterer's nail

enamel paint

varnish

Spinning Top

Handle: 1 off 10 × 3 ×⅞ in (250 × 75 × 21 mm) hardwood

Top: 1 off 4 ½ in (112.5 mm) to turn to 3½ × 2½ × 2½ in (87.5 × 62.5 × 62.5 mm) hardwood or softwood

Spindle: 1 off 4⅛ × ⅜ in (103 × 9 mm) dowel

Rip cord: 36 in (914 mm) (approx.) off ¹⁄₁₆-⅛ in (1.5-3 mm) cord

Rip-cord handle: 1 off 3 × ½ in (75 × 12.5 mm) dowel

1 upholsterer's nail

enamel paint

varnish

Tools

woodworker's lathe	⅛ in (3 mm) drill
basic woodturning tools	⅜ in (9 mm) drill
tenon saw	half-round smooth file
coping saw	hammer
hand drill	cork rubber
¹⁄₁₆ in (1.5 mm) drill	glasspaper

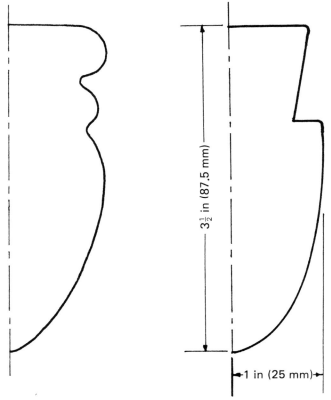

Figure 114

Figure 115

3½ in (87.5 mm)

1 in (25 mm)

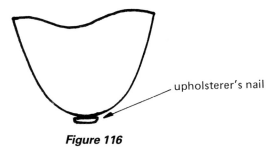

upholsterer's nail

Figure 116

Figure 117

½ in (12.5 mm)

¾ in (18 mm)

⅛ in (3 mm) diameter

The spinning top and whipping top have been old favourites with children for many years. The whipping top requires an element of skill both to set the top in motion and to keep it spinning by using the whip once started. Because the top is fun to play with, coordination naturally develops with its use. These simple but absorbing toys are rugged enough to withstand years of boisterous play. There are many games related to spinning tops which grandparents may be able to remember. To make both the spinning top and the whipping top, you will need access to a woodturning lathe.

Whipping top

The whipping top can be made from either hardwood or softwood. The advantage of hardwood is that it tends to be heavier and will stand up to hard usage. The length of the whipping top is 3½ in (87.5 mm) and it is turned from a suitable piece of wood which is free from knots and measures 2 x 2 in (50 x 50 mm). Mark the ends of the wood with diagonals to find the centres and then set the wood up on the lathe to be turned between centres.

Figures 114 and 115 show two suggested shapes that could be turned, although these designs do not have to be strictly adhered to. You must, however, remember to taper the base of your top to a rounded point. Depending on the length of the piece of wood you are turning, two or three tops can be made at the same time. When you are satisfied with your shape, glasspaper the top to a fine finish. Remove the work from the lathe and saw the waste from the top and bottom; then glasspaper to a good finish in preparation for varnishing.

Counterbore a hole in the base of the top to receive an upholsterer's nail. This will reduce the possibility of the top splitting and will provide a more efficient fulcrum for the whipping top to spin on (figure 116). Apply one or two coats of clear varnish. The top will give even more pleasure if you decorate it with brightly coloured enamel paint. It can then be finished with another coat of clear varnish.

½ in (12.5 mm) squares

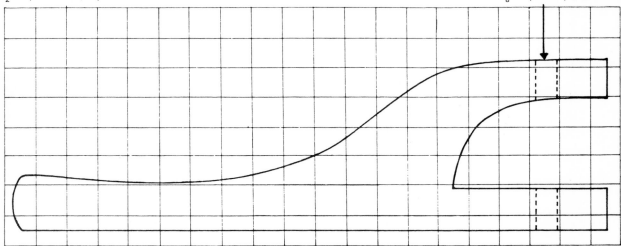
⅜ in (9 mm) diameter

The whip

To make the whip for the top, you will need a piece of ½ in (12.5 mm) dowel 20 in (500 mm) long. Drill a ⅛ in (3 mm) diameter hole ¾ in (18 mm) from one end of the handle (figure 117) to take a piece of cord 36 in (914 mm) long. Glasspaper and varnish the handle. Knot the cord in position on the handle.

Using the whipping top

The whipping top is now ready to be used, ideally on a large, smooth area. Wind the cord around the top to its full length. Hold the whipping top vertically and close to the floor. In the other hand hold the handle of the whip, and flick that hand away from the body. Keep the top spinning by carefully whipping it, to maintain its rate of spin. This may require a little practice at first but is soon mastered.

Spinning top

The spinning top is a more refined version of the whipping top, which does not require so much skill or space to operate. For this top a handle is used, and a spindle is attached to the top, so that it can rotate freely in the arms of the handle. A hole is drilled in the spindle so that a rip cord can be wound around the spindle. The handle is held so that the top is close to the ground, and the rip cord is sharply pulled.

This sets the top spinning and allows the spindle to drop from the handle.

Handle

To make the handle you will need a piece of good-quality hardwood 10 × 3 × ⅞ in (250 × 75 × 21 mm), which is fairly straight-grained and free of knots. Mark the handle out as shown in figure 118. Saw it to shape using a coping saw. Drill a ⅜ in (9 mm) diameter hole vertically through the handle (figure 118). You can if you wish round the handle using a half-round smooth file, so that it fits comfortably into the hand. Clean the handle with glasspaper in preparation for finishing with two or three coats of clear varnish.

Top

The spinning top, like the whipping top, can be made from either hardwood or softwood, but if hardwood is obtainable it is preferable to make the spinning top from this. The top is made from a piece of wood 3½ × 2½ × 2½ in (87.5 × 62.5 × 62.5 mm). Do not forget that the wood needs to be an inch or so longer than the measurements given to allow for the top to be turned between centres on the woodworker's lathe.

Mark both ends of the piece of wood with diagonals and find the centres before setting up the piece of wood on the lathe

Figure 118

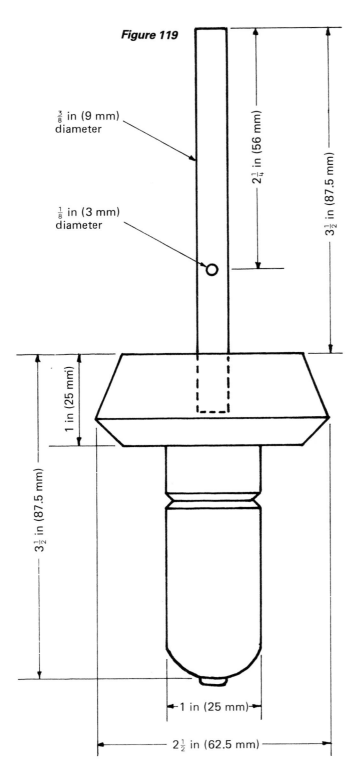

Figure 119

$\frac{3}{8}$ in (9 mm) diameter

$\frac{1}{8}$ in (3 mm) diameter

$2\frac{1}{4}$ in (56 mm)

$3\frac{1}{2}$ in (87.5 mm)

1 in (25 mm)

$3\frac{1}{2}$ in (87.5 mm)

1 in (25 mm)

$2\frac{1}{2}$ in (62.5 mm)

in preparation for turning. The shape and dimensions shown on the top in figure 119 are intended to give the basic proportions of the top. These can be varied slightly to suit your own design. Once the top has been turned to shape, clean it up with glasspaper to give a good finish before removing it from the lathe. Remove the waste from the top and bottom of the spinning top and finish by hand using glasspaper.

Mount the stem of the top in a three-jaw chuck and drill a ⅜ in (9 mm) diameter hole in the centre of the head of the top to a depth of ⅝ in (15 mm). This hole will receive the spindle which is made from a piece of dowel 4⅛ × ⅜ in (103 × 9 mm). Glue the dowel into position in the head of the top as shown in figure 119. Drill a ⅛ in (3 mm) diameter hole through the centre of the dowel 2¼ in (56 mm) from the top of the dowel (figure 119). This hole is to receive the rip cord which will set the top spinning.

Clean up the spindle with glasspaper, so that it rotates freely in the ⅜ in (9 mm) diameter holes in the handle. As in the whipping top, counterbore a hole in the centre of the base of the spinning top to take an upholsterer's nail. Hammer this lightly into position and finish the top with varnish and if you wish, coloured enamel paints.

Rip cord
For the rip cord you will need a piece of good-quality cord, approximately 36 in (914 mm) long and ¹⁄₁₆ in (1.5 mm) in diameter, but certainly no thicker than ⅛in (3 mm) in diameter. The handle of the rip cord is made from a piece of dowel 3 x ½ in (75 x 12.5 mm). Drill the handle in the centre with a ⅛ in (3 mm) drill (figure 120) so that the cord can be threaded through and knotted in position. Using the handle makes the pulling operation to set the top in motion more efficient than just holding the string in the hand, as it allows a more positive action.

Using the spinning top
All you need to do to set your top spinning is to position the top in the handle, thread

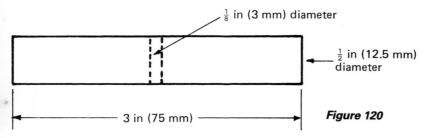

$\frac{1}{8}$ in (3 mm) diameter

$\frac{1}{2}$ in (12.5 mm) diameter

3 in (75 mm)

Figure 120

the cord through the hole in the spindle, wind the cord onto the spindle by turning the top, and pull sharply.

Conversion Table

The models in this book were made using imperial measurements and for ease of reading, the following metric equivalents are given in the text and diagrams.

If you are working in metric, it will be necessary for the accuracy of the working models to use an exact conversion from the imperial measurements to metric, as given below.

Inches	Millimetres	Inches	Millimetres
1/32	0.75	1/32	0.794
1/16	1.5	1/16	1.588
3/32	2.25	3/32	2.381
1/8	3	1/8	3.175
3/16	4.5	3/16	4.762
1/4	6	1/4	6.35
5/16	7.5	5/16	7.938
3/8	9	3/8	9.525
13/32	9.75	13/32	10.319
1/2	12.5	1/2	12.7
9/16	13.5	9/16	14.278
5/8	15	5/8	15.875
3/4	18	3/4	19.05
7/8	21	7/8	22.225
15/16	22.5	15/16	23.802
1	25	1	25.4

Index